The Fourth Resource

 THE ASSOCIATION FOR INFORMATION MANAGEMENT

Aslib, The Association for Information Management, has some two thousand corporate members worldwide. It actively promotes better management of information resources.

Aslib lobbies on all aspects of the management of and legislation concerning information. It provides consultancy and information services, professional development training, conferences, specialist recruitment, and the Aslib Internet Programme and publishes primary and secondary journals, conference proceedings, directories and monographs.

Further information about Aslib can be obtained from:

Aslib, The Association for Information Management,
Information House, 20–24 Old Street, London ECIV 9AP, United Kingdom.
Tel: +44 171 253 4488, Fax: +44 171 430 0514, Email: aslib @ aslib.co.uk
WWW:http://www.aslib.co.uk/aslib/

The Fourth Resource

Resource

INFORMATION AND ITS MANAGEMENT

edited by

David P Best

Published by
Aslib/Gower
Gower House
Croft Road
Aldershot
Hampshire GU11 3HR
England

Gower
Old Post Road
Brookfield
Vermont 05036
USA

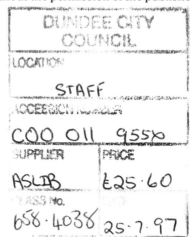

British Library Cataloguing in Publication Data

Fourth Resource: Information and Its
Management
 I. Best, David
 658.4038

ISBN 0–566–07696–9

        Library of Congress Cataloging-in-Publication Data

The fourth resource: information and its management/edited by David
 P. Best.
        p.   cm.
    Includes index.
    ISBN 0–566–07696–9
    1. Management information systems. 2. Information resources management. 3. Information technology. 4. Industrial management–Data processing. I. Best, David P.
 HD30.213.F68   1995
 658.4'038—dc20   95–9310
                                                                         CIP

Typeset in Cheltenham by Raven Typesetters, Chester and printed in Great Britain by Biddles Ltd, Guildford

Contents

PART IV   A TRANSATLANTIC PERSPECTIVE

List of Figures

List of contributors

DR DAVID BEST is a partner with Touche Ross Management Consultants and a well known and highly respected figure in consultancy in the UK and in mainland Europe. He is an acknowledged expert in three areas: Business Process Reengineering; Information Management; and Change Management at individual, team and corporate levels.

Between 1993 and 1995 his clients have included: British Gas, British Coal, British Rail, The British Library, British Home Stores, European Bank for Reconstruction and Development, Nationwide Building Society, Mercury Asset Management, Ofgas, Barclays Bank plc, United Nations Organisation – Geneva, World Intellectual Property Organisation, Department of Trade and Industry, Department of Social Services.

He has published and spoken nationally on his specialist subjects, often chairing or providing key note speeches to conferences. He is a Visiting Professor at the University of Strathclyde in the Department of Information Science, and is a Member of the Editorial Board of the *International Journal for Information Management* and editor of this book.

DR BRIAN S. COLLINS holds the position of Head of Information Systems at The Wellcome Trust, the medical research charity, in London, where he is responsible for all information systems activities. In particular, he is involved in generating a network and generic applications infrastructure that will support a set of reliable, manageable, secure, interactive, on-line multimedia information services in support of the Trust's scientific and policy work. He has been an information strategy and security consultant with PCSL and KPMG, following a long career in the scientific civil service that culminated in the position of Director of Science and Technology at GCHQ, where he was responsible for the design, development and operation of a global secure telecommunications network linking a complex set of high performance data processors.

He is a Fellow of the Institute of Electrical Engineers, a Freeman of the Worshipful Company of Information Technologists, and Visiting Professor in

Health Information Policy at the Centre for Health Information and Multicultural Education (CHIME) at University College, London.

BILL COOK is the Partner in Charge of Ernst & Young's Performance Improvement Group for the Public Sector. Bill has a very extensive background in the field of public sector reforms, beginning in the early 1980s with the Financial Management Initiative through Efficiency Scrutinies (under the Rayner banner) and the establishment of agencies, and including leadership of the Cabinet Office/MPO Information Management Group. Since leaving the Civil Service in 1987, Bill has participated in the creation of TECs and the Review of Agency Performance, before becoming involved in the current issues surrounding market testing, outsourcing, fundamental expenditure reviews and efficiency plans.

BLAISE CRONIN is Professor of Information Science at Indiana University, Bloomington, and Dean of the School of Library and Information Science. From 1985–1991 he was Professor of Information Science and Head of the Department of Information Science, University of Strathclyde, Glasgow. Dr. Cronin has published extensively in the areas of strategic information management, citation analysis, and information marketing. He has taught, researched or consulted in more than 30 countries. His consulting clients have included the World Bank, Asian Development Bank, Hewlett-Packard (Ltd) UK, British Library, Unecsco, and the British Council. Professor Cronin is a Fellow of the Institute of Information Scientists and the Institute of Management.

CLIVE HOLTHAM of Bull Information Systems is Professor of Information Management, City University Business School. After studying at Oxford and Birmingham Universities, Clive trained as an accountant. He was Young Accountant of the Year in 1976 and, after working in financial systems and planning, was a director of finance and information technology from 1982–88.

The focus of his professional post is the strategic application of IT to business problems. In 1989, the Business School created one of the world's first MBA courses specifically focused on Information Technology and Management. This course subsequently was awarded first prize in the British Computer Society's Award for Excellence in IT Management.

Holtham is the inventor of the Business Facilitation System (BFS), which forms a £500 000 research project co-funded by industrial collaborators under the UK government's Computer Supported Cooperative Work Programme. He was an active member of the EC-funded BPR research programme (COBRA), and is a founding member of City University's unique multi-disciplinary, multi-school BPR Research Group.

He has had over 100 articles published, and is the author of several books including *Executive Information Systems and Decision Support* (Chapman and Hall, 1992) *IT and Marketing* (Alfred Waller, 1995), *Managing Information* (Open University Press, 1995). His international research study into 'Improving the productivity of workgroups through Information Technology' has been translated into French and widely circulated and quoted. He is a regular speaker at national and international conferences, and appears regularly on television to comment on strategic IT topics.

His consultanty clients have included Lotus, Microsoft, IBM, Britannia Building Society, Arthur Andersen, KPMG, the UK Treasury and Glaxo.

ELIZABETH ORNA is an independent information consultant, writer and lecturer. Her interest in the problem of assigning value to information (the theme of her contribution to *The Fourth Resource*) arises from her work on organizational information policies, which forms the subject of her book *Practical Information Policies* (Gower 1990, 1995).

Her other books include, *Information Handling in Museums* (Library Association 1980), and *Managing Information for Research* (to be published by the Open University Press in 1995).

She is particularly concerned with how information is presented for use in the form of 'information products', and, with the typographer Graham Stevens with whom she has collaborated for many years, she has written on the shared territory between information science and information design.

KARA OVERFELT is a doctoral student in the School of Library and Information Science at Indiana University, Bloomington. She has a BA in Sociology and MLS and MBA degrees from Indiana University. She is currently a Chancellor's Scholar and recipient of a PhD fellowship from the US Department of Education. From 1986–1992 she was Senior Analyst in the Corporate Treasurer's Office of a Fortune 50 company. She has co-authored a number of research articles with Blaise Cronin.

JULIA PARSONS BSc is an IT professional with 25 years' experience. She trained as a programmer and followed the traditional career path from development programming, through systems analysis and project management, to consultancy. As part of a large integrated team, she contributed to the development of International Banking Systems for two major American banks. These were developed using data analysis techniques and structured programming.

Since joining Touche Ross seven years ago, she has extended her IT development and implementation knowledge to include the handling of information in any form. As a result of this work in Information Management, she now leads the special interest group on records and information management and is responsible for the biennial Touche Ross Information Management Survey. She has published several articles and is a frequent speaker on records and information management issues.

BILL THOM is a Scot (born in 1943), who has been involved in the field of document management most of his working life. He qualified as an industrial librarian in the early 1970s and after some time with Shell International and the Greater London Council, where he set up a number of important on-line information retrieval systems, spent two years in Vienna as a documentation adviser to part of the UN. On his return to the UK he spent five years with the English Tourist Board and a further three years with the UK tobacco industry developing advanced computer-based applications with a strong emphasis on unstructured text-based information. In 1986 he joined the supply side of the *xi* business and has remained there ever since in a number of roles. As a former director of Harwell Computer Power and BRS Software Products, companies specializing in text retrieval and information management, he was instrumental in the combination of these technologies and the emerging field of document imaging. He recently joined Interleaf in the UK as their Business Development Manager where he is responsible for a programme to build up Interleaf's collaborative approach to document management projects with leading IT and management consultancies and systems integrators. He is very interested in finding opportunities to combine document management technology with business process transformation to the point where critical documents, currently left outside the business process, 'reside in' or 'become' the process itself.

PETER VICKERS originally trained as an aircraft engineer with the De Havilland Aircraft Company, but after a spell abroad, began a second career in information work. After fourteen years as a practising information scientist, he joined the consultancy service of Aslib in 1967, later becoming head of their Research and Consultancy Division. It was during his early years with Aslib that he became increasingly involved in projects calling for the introduction of corporate information management, rather than the solution of specific systems problems. In 1985, he and his consultancy colleagues formed an independent firm, The Information Partnership. He retired from the Partnership in 1992 and now works as a freelance consultant. During his 27 years as a consultant, he has worked for a wide variety of organizations, in various European and further-flung countries. He has a particular professional interest in the development and application of techniques for mapping information flows in large organizations.

Preface

Why is this book called *The Fourth Resource*? We are accustomed to thinking of our organizations in terms of the three key resources of traditional economics, those of people, money and physical resources. The economic view being that value is created by the interaction of these three. This book's title reflects the recognition among theoreticians and practitioners alike that information now has taken its place as the fourth resource, ranking equally with the other three in importance. If this claim needs justification, consider the effects of lack of information on the financial markets on 'Black Wednesday', or the havoc caused by insider dealing when some individuals have information which others, equally entitled to it, do not.

The examples are many and various; information on adverse drug reactions not being available when needed or not being managed in a way which enabled early warning to patients is another case in point. The lack of international information management in the attempts to stop the drug trade or other aspects of international crime is a further case, and one which gains widespread media attention. This book has been produced to highlight the practical and theoretical challenges facing us if we are to make progress in this vital area.

The book is addressed to two principal audiences:

- the general management audience which is concerned with what to do about actual information in the organization itself, as opposed to the technology which absorbs such substantial time and cost. The relationship of information management to business process and strategy and to information technology, the vexed issue of the worth of information value and the benefits to be gathered from information management are all addressed here;
- the specialist information manager, records manager, archivist or librarian wishing to know where the current thinking is leading should also find much of interest.

The contributors have been drawn from academia, consultancy and practising information managers.

Before describing the structure of the book, however, I should briefly address the question: why bother? Why should information be managed, and what are the benefits for those who do manage it?

Over 94 per cent of our information is on paper, the 6 per cent on computer costs a great deal of money – capital and revenue. The 250 million personal computers (PCs) in use now represent a total cost of ownership of $1250 bn.

Our benchmarking projects have shown benefits from low hundreds of thousands of pounds to two million pounds sterling per annum from the use of information management method and techniques, while our current information management survey shows that over 60 per cent of respondents have to reinvent information because this is quicker than to find it in the mess of information in most organizations. Almost as many respondents feared litigation through not being able to produce information to order.

These examples alone show the necessity of taking active charge of information in the organization, in the same way that we actively manage money, people, and equipment. The objective of this book is to show how the concepts of information management relate to business management value and the application of technology.

Accordingly Part I, Business Management and Information Value, discusses the links between business process and information management and the varying ways of valuing information; as well as the characteristics of the professionals needed to implement information management.

The emergence of the new information professional as advertised in Holtham's chapter will be necessary to bridge the gaps between functional, technology and specialist managers. If this sounds like the hybrid manager, then it probably is, in an extended edition.

The impact for business will be in far greater understanding and appreciation of the link between business purpose and information, and is central to achieving the outcome of a greater ability to control the investment in information technology (IT) to areas of real benefit and to control the cost of non-IT based information processing. The hows and whats of this process are illustrated by Part II, The Technology Angle, where Julia Parsons discusses the scope and applications of process modelling and the tools available for it, while Bill Thom's chapter exemplifies what can be done with specific illustrations from hypertext applications.

Part III, Information Management in the Real World, provides some 'warts and all' discussion of how information management has been applied and some of the problems which are commonly encountered.

Professor Cronin's chapter in Part IV provides a useful foil in describing the experience in the US. Finally I have drawn the conclusions of the work together in a short Conclusion.

I believe that the chapters forming the work make a valuable contribution to the definition and development of this new but exciting field. I and my fellow contributors hope that you will find much of interest and value in it.

David P. Best

Acknowledgements

I am indebted to many colleagues and friends in the development of this book. So many have contributed to the development of my thinking in information management that to name individuals is invidious. I would, however, like to remember the late Paul Martin whose encouragement, wit and insight first caused me to think seriously about the subject. My thanks also go to my fellow contributors, who made my life as editor very straightforward, to my secretary Karen Wake whose forbearance and diligence have contributed enormously to the timely completion of the text and to Anne Guyomar for her retyping of key sections.

DPB

Part I

BUSINESS MANAGEMENT AND INFORMATION VALUE

1 Business process and information management

David P. Best

Following Hammer and Champey's (1993) development of the concept of business process re-engineering (BPR), the attention of management experts and practitioners alike has been drawn to the subject of *process* in business organizations.

In parallel with this, the growth of information management (IM) as a broad subject encompassing all areas of corporate information has been significant in Europe in general and the UK in particular. In the USA, IM as a topic has still been restricted to information resources management and/or librarianship despite the job title of Chief Information Officer at executive level, which is almost entirely restricted in practice to management of the information technology (IT) resources of the corporation despite, in theory, covering all information resources. At the same time, most BPR methods stress the role of IT in the BPR activity while addressing the issues of the information to be managed only obliquely.

This book is about the state of the art in managing information rather than being primarily about technology. Since information management is directed towards managing information to contribute to business performance it is very important to understand what the key areas of business change are which the information manager will have to confront over the next few years. Business process engineering in whatever guise is probably the most significant of these. Consequently this introductory chapter is split into three main sections:

1 a brief overview of the process view of business, which currently forms the main and central plank of analytical thinking about business;
2 a consideration of information management in the context of process;
3 the likely requirements of the information management field over the next several years.

The definition of information management used in this book is taken from the Touche Ross survey (1994) as used by several other bodies notably the UK

Association of Information and Image Management (AIIM) and Cimtech. We define information management as: 'the effective production, storage, retrieval and dissemination of information in any format and on any medium to support business objectives'.

Before outlining what is covered by this definition, it will be useful to start this keynote chapter with an exploration of business process so that we can see clearly the context in which this activity take place.

THE BUSINESS PROCESS VIEW

The world view underlying this section is essentially systems based in the sense of Checkland (1984), Beer (1986, 1991) and views organizations essentially as socio-technical systems, as discussed by Emery and Trist (1960) and Churchman (1968). For practical purposes we may regard a *process* in these terms as: 'the set of resources and activities (whether undertaken by people or by machines) necessary and sufficient to convert some input into some output'.

This view of process is extremely simple, deceptively so: the difference between a 'marketing department' and looking at marketing as a process which results in the creation of opportunities to sell is significant. In the first view one thinks in terms of mounting exhibitions, designing packaging, advertising campaigns and the like as a series of discrete activities. In the latter case one thinks far more in terms of a single, integrated process of action designed to achieve a series of graded objectives each with a measurable criterion of success.

Such a view of organisational purpose and process is still far from commonplace and it is frequently resisted by conservative management on the grounds that it is:

- too theoretical;
- nothing but management by objectives (MBO);
- nothing but organization and methods (O&M) – and, since both are old hat, so is the process view;
- too difficult;
- too easy.

And on any or all of these grounds, process thinking is heavily discounted.

The process view is simple but if life was this simple, would we need BPR and would it have created the storm of interest which it has? We know, to our cost, that in most organizations such a simple view of process is difficult to apply because:

- the organization itself may be highly complex in structure because it is the result of mergers and take-overs as well as of long-term organic growth;
- the crosshatch of geography, function and organization makes it very difficult to observe processes from looking at business structures;

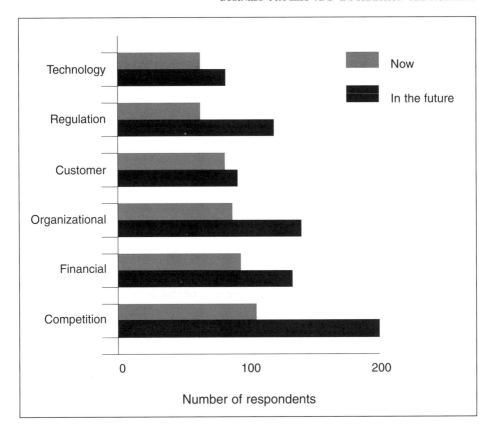

Figure 1.1   Main drivers to change

- computer systems, now representing possibly as many as three generations of technology, may be in place throughout the business and will themselves mirror the complexity of the organization.

All of these factors combine to make it difficult to discern the few, often quite straightforward, processes which underlie this complexity. All too often managerial and consulting effort is applied to the complexity, rather than to the fundamentals of the business.

Why do organizations undertake BPR? Mainly as a response to the pressure to change. Figure 1.1 shows the main drivers to change from a survey of 250 executives undertaken by Jeans (1994). This shows that competition is by far the greatest driver for change, followed by financial, organizational and regulatory pressure. Interestingly, customer pressure and technology are at the bottom of this league though, arguably, regulation acts as a surrogate customer in many sectors.

Process Re-engineering versus process improvement

What is the difference between these two terms? The first, very much advocated by Hammer and Champey, implies a top-down, revolutionary redesign of   5 all processes in the business, beginning with the objective/mission of the organization and working from that through to implementing completely revised processes, supported by new organizational structures and systems. This has been very much the US approach and it has some successes and some failures to its credit. A Business Intelligence special report (1993) claims that survey research shows that some 50–70 per cent of BPR projects fail to deliver dramatic benefits.

The second process is a more European approach, advocated by, among others, Clive Holtham at City University Business School, and focuses much more on the concept of process rationalization and improvement. This takes a much more incremental approach to BPR. The broad features of both are described below.

In the radical version of BPR the process runs as follows:

1 Set out clearly the organization's mission or purpose.
2 Establish the need for change.
3 Build a model of the process needed to meet these objectives.
4 Design the physical process, taking account of the opportunity for the use of technology and skilled people.
5 Implement the change, with all the necessary attention to communication, training, testing, quality management etc., that is required.

It is noticeable that this series of events makes no mention of the current processes. This is because in 'pure' BPR no account is taken of the way things are currently carried out. The emphasis is on radical redesign.

In the majority of cases reported, for example in the journal *Business Change and Reengineering,* the approach has been rather less radical. In these cases the approach has focused on first understanding the present process in the

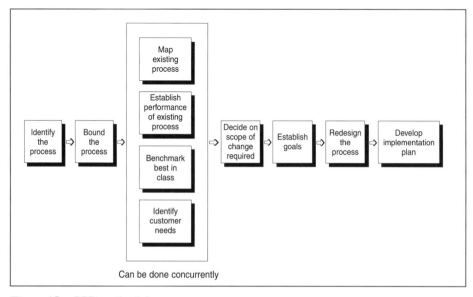

Figure 1.2   BPR methodology

context used to inform the redesign. Figure 1.2 shows an example of the methodology which illustrates this way of approaching BPR. The emphasis is very much more on analysing and assessing the current process. The results of the analysis are then examined in the light of the purpose of the process, its outputs and the associated service levels. In the majority of cases this shows a gap between the desired and the actual, in terms of service levels, output quality and the effectiveness of the underlying purposes. The remaining steps are tasks aimed at rationalizing, structuring, and improving the process so as to eliminate the gap between the actual process and the desired process.

In both approaches the process of analysis is complemented by process modelling techniques, work measurement and job design, and by system analysis methods. In many cases this incremental approach to processes is more easily accepted by members of organizations and is less dramatic in its effects, but without necessarily being less effective.

Whither the process view?

The purpose of introducing this subject in a book on information management is that the process view is at present the predominant way of looking at organizations. I believe that this is likely to remain so for the foreseeable future for a number of reasons:

1   Process provides a logically rigorous view of the relationship between inputs and outputs.
2   This view is quite separate from organizational structure, which can be defined in a variety of ways to achieve the same process result.
3   Seeing the transactions of the business within a process framework facilitates deciding where automation is appropriate.
4   The process view also facilitates the identification of the most appropriate role of each of the four main categories of resource, namely people, money, machinery, and information.

On each of these counts the process view is here to stay and, in common with many other disciplines, information managers are going to have to accommodate this approach within their world view. Furthermore, as I hope to show below, the essential nature of the role which information plays in business, that is, the role of information in process, is not well enough understood. This has led to:

● massive information overload at all levels (90 per cent of managers claim to have too much paper);
● frequently ineffective use of IT, with unrealized benefits and cost overruns;
● poor decision-making;
● lack of retention or of corporate learning;
● loss of profits.

In the next section, I examine the role of information from the process viewpoint to identify the emerging aspects of IM which are particular to the process approach. But as background, the following problems from our 1994 survey are striking:

- 69 per cent of respondents complained that they and colleagues kept vital information to themselves despite the problems of paper overload;
- 65 per cent suffered constraints in strategic space;
- 61 per cent found information difficult to find, or not in the right form;
- 59 per cent had to re-create information because they could not find it or because the form was inappropriate;
- 51 per cent suffered from missing or lost information.

Against this background is any further evidence required that effective information management is urgently required to avoid the costs involved in the problems noted above?

INFORMATION AND ITS MANAGEMENT

In this section I outline some of the features of information management today with a view then to examining some of the features of information from the process standpoint.

Information management today

The Touche Ross & Co. (1994) *Information Management Survey* (first conducted in 1992), shows that the problems of IM have not lessened over the period between the two surveys; the amount of paper has decreased slightly as shown by Figure 1.3 but the problem has now shifted to that of retrieval.

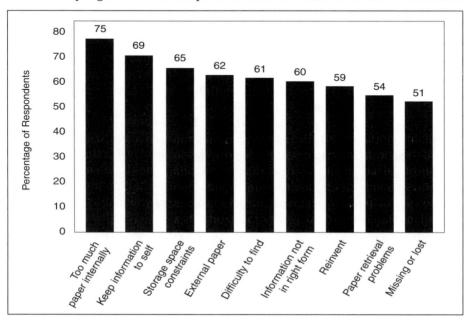

Figure 1.3   Problems experienced

Having automated the chaos it seems that the needle has been finally lost, not in the haystack but in the machine.

Equally the role of records management is no better understood and the records manager is not necessarily any more involved in the automation of records-related functions than before. On the other hand the proceedings of the Records Management Society (RMS) and other professional bodies do not reflect any greater concern with the issues of the wider corporate world than when the survey was first undertaken. Why is this?

I think the answer lies to some extent in the fragmentation of the profession, and I comment further on this below. Fragmentation has made it easy for professional information managers of all persuasions to confine their attention to the narrow domain, for example the archive or the registry, the library or the information centre, and thus miss the significance of their activity to the achievement of wider business goals. For this impact to be better understood it is necessary for the information manager to be able to see the role which information plays in the business process and hence where their own function fits in the context of the whole.

Information in business process

If we examine the range of business processes from an IM standpoint, we can see quickly that there are two major divisions to the role which information plays in business process:

1   Where information is the raw material and subject of the process, for example Social Security or credit card activity, investment activity, research grant funding, the Arts etc.;
2   Where information facilitates the process by way of allowing control, monitoring, oversight etc., for example in accounting systems or manufacturing.

There is a clear distinction to be made here between the former type which is information intrinsic to the process and the latter type which is extrinsic to it:

● *Intrinsic information* is the information which is itself the subject and object of the process. In the assessment of eligibility for benefit the information about the claimant is itself the basis of the decision and determines the outcome; in investment and fund management activity the timeliness and accuracy of the information as well as the confidence in it is a critical factor as to the effectiveness of the decision reached using it.
● *Extrinsic information* is not the subject of the process but provides the means whereby the process can be controlled. In this case the information is ancillary to the process. Examples of this would be stock systems and manufacturing systems where, although the information provided has a fundamental role to play, the outcome of the process can proceed without it, albeit at lower levels of efficiency.

What is the significance for IM of this distinction? I believe it is a fundamental one. In the case of extrinsic information we are dealing mainly with
measurement of or data about the underlying process which could proceed
without the information albeit at a much reduced level of efficiency, economy
and performance. In the case of intrinsic information, however, not only is
information used to control the process but the process itself is comprised of
information as input, processed material and output.

Information management of information-based processes

In this situation the behaviour of the people carrying out the process is
behaviour related intrinsically to the information content of the task. Share
dealing is probably the most graphic example of this class by virtue of the
monetary value associated with the information and also by virtue of the fact
that the process cannot continue without the information and is dependent on
it, as Black Wednesday so graphically illustrated: when the dealing room
systems stopped under the volume of information flooding through the
world's markets, so did dealing.

In this class of process not only is the information itself not structured to the
same extent as is data, but the processes to which it relates, because they are
often intellectual or subjective and value based, are also not articulated
clearly or understood analytically. This is particularly true of the lower finan-
cially valued information processes. Though even in the financial services
sector there are processes which are only now beginning to be clearly explicated in terms of the information activity which they involve, as the history
of the ill-fated Taurus project showed. This distinction again forces us to
examine the process–information link so that we can better understand what
IM can contribute to the efficiency of process.

Interestingly, even in these processes information is only the preponderant
resource, not the only resource. We can see clearly that the process has as its
main *raison d'être* the provision of an output which consists of information,
but that there are other significant and important non-information assets
being employed.

In these cases we need all the skills of the professional information manager
not only to help colleagues obtain the raw material of the process, and to help
them to make best use of it, but also, taking the process view, information
management is needed to help understand the processes by which they convert the raw information received into the decision, report or other output.

This is true not only for the direct subject of the information-based process
but also for the surrounding, less structured, information. For example, a fund
management organization used the skills of their information managers and IT
staff in combination to put together information on the financial markets from
on-line and published sources, together with informal information, to provide
a global village of managed information to better serve their clients. They were
only able to do this through pooling their joint skills to better understand the
process of serving clients in a global market from an IM and IT perspective.

The head office of a multinational organization used intellectual property
rights experts, information and records managers, and IT specialists to

BUSINESS PROCESS AND INFORMATION MANAGEMENT

implement a framework of policy and practice for the secretariat based upon an understanding of their processes which emerged through the dialogue of these three groups.

In both examples the perspective of the information manager was central to arriving at a good and robust model of the process in information terms.

Extrinsic information

As a consequence of the control and command purpose of this type of information, the information is often numerical or 'hard' data with small amounts of descriptive text, and the management of it is often related closely to the underlying physical activity. This is the type of information which has been most readily computerized, and the context and nature of which is best understood by those outside the IM disciplines.

So-called decision support tools, executive information systems and similar technologies act to facilitate the summarization, interpretation and extrapolation of computer-based management information but there has been little formal understanding of the unstructured information used in the control and decision process, for example today's background from the *Financial Times*, the Board Room 'gossip' and reports, circulars etc. The latest Department of Trade and Industry (DTI) initiative, Computer Supported Co-operative Work (CSCW) programme, in some measure is an attempt to rectify this in the UK context, but it is still focused primarily on the technological components of the processes rather than on the information content.

The role of information management

There is plenty of scope therefore for the profession to move out into the wide process world to merge their skills with those of other professions.

Certainly in either of the two categories of information process there are a number of conditions which as information managers we are in a position to see satisfied and which, if met, would undoubtedly improve the clarity of information management, in particular:

- the relationship between the item of information and the output and control of the process needs to be demonstrable;
- the results of the information not being available should be capable of expression as a quantified impact (or some subjective surrogate agreed by the stakeholder);
- such categories of information should be capable of a ranking in priority order.

These criteria, though apparently commonsensical, have rarely been applied rigorously to information in business whether the information is paper or computer based. If they had been it is probable that the amount of paper kept would be significantly less and that the success and cost benefit of many computer systems would have been improved (see also Best, 1989).

Once the three criteria have been satisfied, there are a number of measures   *11* which can be implemented to ensure the regular and systematic provision of information at levels of quality acceptable to the business. These measures are once again old hat to the 'traditional' information manager, but appear not to be applied at business level throughout the economy. Our studies of 'best of breed' in IM show that these measures have been implemented by the 'best' companies, but by few others.

The measures include:

- *Policies*. For example is all information a corporate asset, or is individual ownership allowed? What are the policies on document naming and classification? Who rules on the sharing of information?
- *Standards*. Are files registered? What standards are used for manual and electronic filing? Are common word processing packages in use throughout the business so that (universally standardized named) files can be easily transferred and recognized?
- *Procedures*. Are there any? Who trains the staff? Is there a quality system which applies to the information management function? Do the procedures enforce the policies on classification, indexing, evaluation of information sources?
- *Technology*. Does the information systems (IS) strategy cover all of the information resources of the organization including paper, image, microfilm and electronic forms, in a prioritized fashion, recognizing the satisfaction of the three criteria set out earlier? Is the definition of levels of benefit consistent with this? Does the post holder responsible for the IS Department actually recognize the necessity of an integrated approach to all the information assets of the business?

Each of the above covers the familiar territory of information managers who are used to addressing questions such as: Who owns and is responsible for the maintenance of the records and flow of information? What is the retention period, what naming and indexing conventions should be applied? What frequency of update is needed, what level of integrity and accuracy should be applied? Notice that many of the questions are also asked and answered by IT professionals in the context of data processing application systems, but here we are seeking to apply similar strict rationality to the 94 per cent of information which is still retained and used in paper form, on microfilm, in word processing systems and as image.

When we have answered these questions we can hope to be able to determine not only the role which such information plays in the management of our businesses but also its value, and hence whether it is worth automating and at what cost in financial and human resources.

Whether the information we are managing is intrinsic to the business process or extrinsic to it, the information manager of the future will need to meet a number of requirements and these are discussed below.

REQUIREMENTS FOR THE FUTURE OF IM IN A PROCESS WORLD

Understanding the resource

Despite the efforts of information managers over the last 15 years, there is still a lack of understanding in general management about the role that information plays in business processes. This is far less true of data, where the data forms a part of the process of the business, for example financial transactions, accounting or share deals, stock movements or information related to stock control and manufacturing processes. The role of unstructured information in management processes, however, or the role of informal information 'gossip' as in business intelligence and similar areas of activity, is still understood, at best, informally and instinctively. In both cases the understanding has been led by technological developments, for example the first wave of accounting systems and the later wave of knowledge-based systems and groupware.

The first major challenge for information managers of the future, therefore, is to discover ways in which the role of information in business process and management can be more clearly articulated as suggested in the previous sections. This poses quite a challenge.

A previous section emphasized the great importance of understanding processes; simply put, if information management is to mean anything in the years to come *it must address the issue of the use of information in the context of the process.* To do this it may be necessary to use the techniques of knowledge engineers to understand more clearly how to *elicit knowledge,* that is, to understand how information is used in a specific context of action or decision-making. It may be appropriate to sit with managers to identify the ways in which they access the various sources of information which they use on a day-to-day basis; to categorize the distinction between formal and informal sources of information; to see how information garnered from the business pages of the *Financial Times* or from the professional press is used together with specific data from the sales force or from the marketing department to inform particular business decisions. This in turn will need to be incorporated into the corporate information memory so that no learning is lost. A number of organizations including Touche Ross and Andersen Consulting are already in the process of implementing such integrated systems.

In turn these types of systems must deliver clear benefits if they are to justify the significant effort and investment involved. This implies ways of valuing information, methods which at present are not well established or well known. This book addresses this subject.

This type of endeavour will require us to find new ways of classifying information to make fine distinctions between formal and informal sources and categories of information. It will require us to refine our indexing methods so as to be better able to mirror and represent the way in which management and staff access information from a wide range of sources. IM will require us also to make our existing indexing schema and our ways of describing information more accessible to those who use it, and it will require a dialogue to be established between the information technologist, the librarian, and information scientists so that over the coming years a shared discourse and shared understanding can be arrived at.

Valuing the asset

One of the major problems historically has been that of assigning an objective or subjective value to the information resource. Various methods have been tried and some of the authors represented in this book are among those who have contributed most to this issue to date. However, it is true that there is still no commonly accepted and universally applicable way of valuing the information resource. Various surrogate measures are used such as the value of the investment in IT used to hold the information, or the staff cost associated with collecting and maintaining it, or the value which it has when it is put to a specific use. Each of these surrogates has its place and its role to play and it may be that in many cases an indirect valuation is all that can be aimed at. The work of Paul Strassman (1985) is a good example of contributions in this area.

However, we do need to develop common standards, formats and agreed methods of representing the value of information so that similar cases in different circumstances can be assessed and compared, and so that we can begin to develop a body of knowledge and expertise about the use and value of information in different contexts. Work on the economics of IT is going on in several academic institutions, for example at the University of Bath, the London Business School and the London School of Economics. This is worthwhile but it needs to be clearly understood what the relationship is between the technology and the information which it supports. These academic initiatives then need to be implemented as practical methods and guidance so that we have ways of accounting for information in the way we have for raw material, plant and equipment, and so on.

The question of what is a library worth, or what is market intelligence worth or is it worth while maintaining subscriptions to 15 or 25 professional and sector journals at the moment can only be answered by the variable and subjective emotive judgement of the person responsible for that particular budget. We must aim towards a system where, even if our valuations are subjective, they are sufficiently well understood and explicated so that we can debate them and form a view as to their extent and acceptability.

The development of such an understanding will be an important element of our increasing knowledge about and understanding of how information can help us to improve our business performance. This in turn will help us to improve the ways in which technology can support information-based tasks.

So far, research on the productivity of white-collar workers who are using IT extensively, has shown that in the majority of cases their productivity is not improved significantly, and in some cases has declined. There are a number of reasons for this, a lack of the understanding of the role of information in management process being a key factor, but it is undoubtedly true that our inability to allocate value to information in process and our lack of understanding about the real nature of information transactions has led to the expenditure of investment funds in an inappropriate or less than ideally appropriate way.

The old adage that if you can measure something, you understand it, is particularly applicable to this area and IT manufacturers, suppliers and library sciences information managers have to accept that, in the long-term interests of the industry, a fuller understanding of how information economics work will be essential if the confidence of the market is to be maintained.

The role of skilled people

One main drawback of the way in which information management has developed in North America and the UK is that, because it has often been seen as the province of the records manager or the librarian, it has correspondingly often been put within the company secretarial department, the administration function or the office services function and has rarely been integrated with the IT department. This has given rise to a separation of management development, training needs, and effectiveness between, on the one hand, the IT department concerned with computerization of data and on the other, the library and records departments which are concerned with the management of paper-based, unstructured, information.

The profession has split broadly into:

● records managers;
● archivists;
● specialist and generalist librarians;
● on-line specialists;

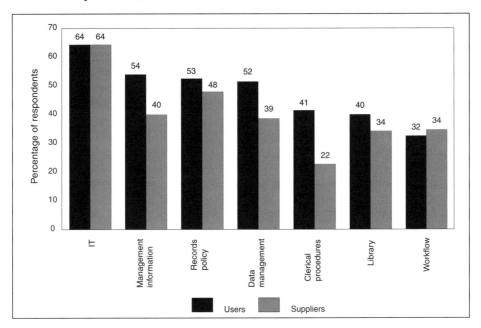

Figure 1.4   Understanding what information management is

- knowledge engineers;
- publishing specialists;
- IT practitioners.

I believe that these communities of interest must become fully integrated over the coming years if the profession is to fulfil its potential to contribute to the effective use of information in business, because all the skills of these disparate groups are needed to understand how information is used.

This raises particular challenges for the future of information management. As Figure 1.4 shows, there is a good deal of confusion in the minds of managers about the nature of information management and who should be responsible for it and therefore a significant number of barriers to be overcome if we are to move information management forward with confidence into its third decade.

What then are the challenges that confront us? They are first of all to improve the awareness of the concept of information management in industry. This needs to involve academics, consultants and the professional bodies through the medium of surveys, books and publications, conferences and exhibitions. Specifically we need to obtain far wider acceptance of the compatibility of information management with IT and data processing in a way which enables the owners and managers of organizations to understand information clearly as a fourth resource, to be managed and controlled in much the same way as any other resource and with its own technology, professional vocabulary, disciplines and skills. An article in the *Records Management Bulletin* (Penn, 1994) and the commentary on the article by the American Specialist Dr J. Michael Pemberton show precisely how far there is to go in this area.

Second, we need to bring together in the information management arena individuals with skills in business analysis and knowledge, ability in information technology, the economics of information and skilled in its application to form the multi-disciplinary teams which are so necessary to an effective application of the concepts. There are a number of these areas of skill which are particularly significant.

Business analysis and process modelling are key to the task of improving the application of information management ideas to improve corporate performance. Until, and unless, we as information managers can represent the role of information in process we will always be accused of being peripheral to the main thrust of business performance.

We need to be able to illustrate and demonstrate to management the way in which less structured information is used in decision-making, in process performance and in sales and marketing so that the role of information management can be clearly identified and the current confusion over the use of information in these contexts eliminated. Equally, familiarity with IT, particularly the enabling technologies (for example full text retrieval, multi-media and image processing applications, knowledge-based systems and neural net computing), will be essential if the effective management and then automation of unstructured information in business process is to be undertaken.

Skills in indexing, classification, parsing, structured vocabulary and thesaurus development, which are the bread and butter of the library sciences end of the information management spectrum, have to be fully integrated with the data analysis, specification and design skills intrinsic to IT if the full power of information management is to be brought to bear in improving business performance. Research by the Nolan Norton group in 1992–93 showed clearly that for the vast majority of IT investment, demonstrable benefit and return on that investment is very hard to come by.

Finally, the multi-disciplinary team also needs to include individuals with understanding and a track record in the application of technology to large projects. We need to enable the development of much stronger professional representation for information managers of all persuasions. Apart from the Association of Information and Image Management in the US and its off-shoot in the UK and the work of Aslib, the Association for Information Management, there is no all-party professional body advocating, and responsible for, the information management area. There needs to be a body of wide appeal to attract professionals from each aspect of the information management spectrum, from the IT analysts through to the specialist research librarian and encompassing all shades of records management, image processing specialists and librarians *en route*. The ideal vehicle for this is difficult to describe, but certainly there needs to be a much greater attempt made to broaden the appeal of the existing professional organizations and to raise the awareness of information management generally.

REFERENCES

Beer, S. (1966), *Decision and Control*, London: John Wiley.
Beer, S. (1986), *Brain of the Firm*, London: John Wiley.
Beer, S, (1991), *The Heart of Enterprise 1991*, London: John Wiley.
Best, D.P. (1989), 'The Future of Information Management', in *IDPM Year Book*, London: Institute of Data Processing Managers.
Business Intelligence (1993), *BPR Management Today Special Report*, London.
Checkland, P. (1984), *Systems Thinking Systems Practice* (repr. 1993), London: John Wiley.
Churchman, C.W. (1968), *The Systems Approach*, New York: Dell.
Emery, F. and Trist, G. (1976), *Systems Thinking*, London: Penguin.
Hammer, J. and Champey, J. (1993), *Reengineering the Corporation*, London: Nicholas Briarley.
Holtham, C. (1993), 'BPR Hype or Reality' (unpublished paper).
Jeans, M. (1994), 'Change, the Pressures and Management's Response', *Business Change and Reengineering*, 1 (3), London: Wiley.
Penn, I. (1994), 'Records Management Professionals: Suffering from Self-Inflicted Wounds', *Records Management Bulletin*, (62), June, London: RMS.
Proc, M., Drew, S. and Wensley, A. (1994), 'The Premier of Ontario's Correspondence Unit Strategic Redesign of the Communication Process', in *Business Change and Reengineering*, 1 (3).
Strassman, P. (1985), *Information Pay-Off*, London: John Wiley.
Touche Ross and Co. (1994), *Information Management Survey*, London: Touche Ross and Co.

2 Valuing information: problems and opportunities

Elizabeth Orna

Having discussed the business issues and the links to process in the last paper, this chapter considers the vexed question of information value and information economics. Elizabeth Orna is a highly respected and experienced professional, and in this wide-ranging overview addresses one of the most difficult topics in the information management field.

This excellent chapter shows clearly why the value of information is so often played down in favour of business cases for the technology which carries it, and why it is that the discipline of information management has so far to go. However, it also provides a number of possible solutions on how to value information and shows the large number of lines of enquiry which have been and are being pursued.

This is an appropriate time to be considering how we set a value on information. On the one hand there is a good deal of loose talk and writing about 'Information, the Fourth Resource', global networks, and the Information Highway, combined with insistence on 'value for money'; on the other, a more sober realization that information – more richly defined than has been the case in the past – is more important than IT, and a concern with reliable valuation of the intangible assets of business – including information. And there are developments in the technology which can at last give some promise of supporting a proper valuation of intangibles.

DEFINITIONS AND THEIR IMPLICATIONS

Value (*Shorter Oxford Dictionary*)

I 1 That amount of some commodity, medium of exchange, etc., which is considered to be an equivalent for something else; a fair or adequate equivalent or return.

2 The material or monetary worth of a thing; the amount at which it may be estimated in terms of some medium of exchange or other standard of a like nature.

II   2   The relative status of a thing, or the estimate in which it is held, according to its real or supposed worth, usefulness, or importance.

The key terms in these definitions are: 'considered', 'estimated', 'relative', 'equivalent for something else', 'medium of exchange or other standard', and 'estimate according to real or supposed worth'. So fixing a value is always an indirect process that involves finding appropriate equivalents and standards, not necessarily or always in money terms, and the estimation of those who use it has to be taken into account as well.

These features of the concept of value explain why the process of valuing is a difficult one.

Valuing

We can define the functional part of valuing fairly simply:

● The process of determining and applying appropriate criteria for esti-mating the value of things.

But the actual business of determining appropriate criteria is hard intel-lectual work, in which both thinking and feeling are involved, and in which conflicting interests can play a part; while the application of the criteria so as to arrive at a reliable evaluation can be a complex process where multiple criteria are involved (as they are in the organizational context) – so complex as to be beyond the unaided capacity of the human memory.

Matters are not helped by the general lack of acquaintance (in the UK at least) with the science of evaluation – axiology[1] or the unified theory of value – which

> provides a methodology within which value problems can be treated and resolved, but is itself independent of the value arguments: the value perspectives in the mind of the decision-maker are separated from the supporting evaluation framework ... the analysis is logical and neutral while the perspectives of the decision-maker and stakeholders can be partisan (McPherson, 1991, p. 1).

Information

The definition of information is perhaps less conventional, but it arises from experience, has proved useful in practice, has a sound theoretical foundation – see, for example, Brookes (1980) and Ingwersen (1992) – and today is widely accepted.

● What we take in from outside to feed our knowledge[2] so that we can func-tion successfully and achieve our aims.
● What is necessary and what is available in given situations for this pur-pose.

This definition of information takes account of some of the peculiarities and unique features which distinguish it from other material resources:

- In order to have value, information has to be transformed by human cognitive processes into human knowledge, without which no products of tangible value can be produced or exchanged.
- Where inflows of the information necessary to maintain knowledge and support appropriate action are blocked, disaster can follow, either quickly (as in aircraft disasters or catastrophic failures in chemical processes), or in the form of a gradual run-down into incompetence and chaos (as in organizations which are grossly mismanaged, underfinanced and understaffed).
- If it is hoarded for the exclusive use of a limited number of people, it can actually fail to achieve its full potential value for those who hoard it, but if it is exchanged and traded, the value resulting from its use increases for all parties to the transactions (see p. 29 for research which indicates that active use of information promotes innovation and allows survival in times of turbulence).
- Information has no inherent value of itself. 'Its value lies in its use' (Abell, 1993, p. 53); 'value is derived from and is added to by those involved with the process of its transfer ... its ultimate value derives entirely from the perception of its recipient and user as to what benefits they see accruing from its provision' (Akeroyd, 1991, p. 89). The parable of the talents is applicable to it.
- Information is a diffused resource, that enters into all the activities of businesses and forms a component of all products and services that are sold. As McPherson (1994a, p. 203) puts it, 'Information permeates all organizations; it is the raw material of cognitive activity ... and ... the means whereby the organization obtains its window on the world.' It also has the paradoxical quality of being usable for measuring the value of other things, but not of itself (ibid.).

WHY THERE ARE PROBLEMS IN VALUING INFORMATION

The definition of information also explains why valuing information is such a knotty problem that most businesses have been content with rather simplistic assumptions, and comparatively few researchers have given it attention.

In the first place, what constitutes information will differ according to the purposes of the individuals or organizations concerned. What is of vital interest to one is of no interest or value to another. Few businesses realize this and few set about defining what information means for them; most are content with rather thin and poverty-stricken definitions, if they attempt the task at all. The argument between the duck and the mouse in *Alice's Adventures in Wonderland* has a message here:

'Found *what?*' said the Duck.
'Found it,' the Mouse replied rather crossly: 'of course you know what "it" means.'

'I know what "it" means well enough when *I* find a thing,' said the Duck: 'it's generally a frog or a worm.'

The failure to recognize the need for an organization-specific definition of information in relation to who needs to use it and for what purposes, makes it difficult if not impossible to develop appropriate criteria for valuing information. The next obstacle is that information at the point of application, unlike other resources used by businesses, is intangible, because it has to be transformed into knowledge inside human minds before it can be applied. Information thus has potential as process as well as product.

Then there is the fact that information is a combination of 'containers' and content; the only hard figure readily available is what we pay for the container/content package (e.g. periodical subscriptions, CD-ROMs, on-line services). It is not common practice to separate content from container when assessing costs and benefits; traditional accounting is not equipped to look at the multiple repeated uses of the content, or to trace the processes of adding value once it is transformed to human knowledge and applied.

The failure to recognize the importance of content and the human transformation of information to knowledge is compounded by the tendency to identify 'information' with 'information technology'. And that is compounded yet further by contemporary disenchantment with the results of investment in IT, and realization of its failure to bring the proposed benefits as against the all too evident costs (though the failure mainly arises from confounding information with IT, and from allowing the technology to be master instead of servant).

And finally, as Poirier (1990, p. 266) points out, the concept of information as a resource like energy or water is not a sustainable analogy, because it doesn't always obey the laws of physics: it is diffuse, compressible and extendable; it can be shared or consumed more than once; it is long-lasting and does not necessarily decrease with use; and it can substitute for other resources, e.g. labour or capital.

So, it is hardly surprising if most businesses have either not tackled the problem at all, or have been content to assess the costs of information in fairly crude terms and to limit their estimate of its value to just those cases where information can actually be packaged and sold. There is probably unawareness, also, of the methods that do exist for expressing the value of intangibles in acceptable and well-founded equivalents. (Yet a comparable problem regularly gets solved in practical circumstances in establishing the relative values of different jobs for purposes of pay decisions.)

McPherson (1994a) gives a useful exposition of some of the existing methods. He also proposes three models of information/information processes which are relevant to the points just discussed. The first relate to the cognition process, by which information enhances the 'state of knowledge' – here the value criteria depend on the contributions which information makes towards achieving external operational and organizational objectives. The second takes into account the fact that 'any resulting value added inside the human brain is not realized until it is converted into some form of external activity that works towards the achievement of recognizable objectives' (cf the approach of Burk and Horton, 1988). '... each and every part and function in an organization must justify its existence by virtue of its contributions to the cost-effective achievement of the organization's existence, survival and objectives' (McPherson, 1994a, p. 207). Model 3 is conventional value added accounting, which 'misses the vital contributions provided by information and knowledge work' (ibid. p. 204) because it is cost oriented and so cannot recognize the output value of knowledge and information processes if output is consumed internally – it can only recognize value if output is sold externally (ibid. p. 208).

Can you value information by applying traditional economic theory?

Some of the characteristics of information which have just been discussed seem to suggest that the answer to this question may be 'No'. But that has not deterred economists from trying over the last 30 years or so.

The economist most often quoted in this context is probably Machlup. He makes a useful distinction between information as process and information as 'content or knowledge' (Machlup, 1979), but is cautious as to the possibility of arriving at a quantitative assessment of the social benefits and costs of information, and downright discouraging on the prospect of valuing it in money terms, or of quantifying the use made of any piece of information. He does, however, regard the use of information as a process of transforming it into knowledge (ibid. p. 246) – which suggests a cognitive approach on the lines described earlier in this chapter (see pp. 19–20).

Brinberg (1989) looks back over the history of attempts to apply conventional economic theory to valuing information: 'Stigler's pioneering article on "The economics of information" published in 1961 stimulated economists to apply traditional economic theory to information and to develop a framework for assessing the value of information' (p. 60). But alas, 'Practical results from these cerebral undertakings have yet to be seen' (ibid.). According to Brinberg, the fundamental assumptions of economic theory account for this – if you try to apply them to information, it is not possible to make 'a logical transition to the real world' (ibid.).

He gives as reasons some of the factors already mentioned, like the running together of information and IT, and the fact that information is dynamic and changing and dependent for its definition on the needs of its users. He adds the further point that information is not a 'fungible' product or resource: there is no obvious measure of a unit of information; its uniqueness 'precludes construction of the traditional demand or supply curves'; and transactions involving information are not usually by direct purchase – they occur at 'one or more stages removed from the user' (ibid.).

So Brinberg too takes the view that 'the true function of information is to be a catalyst. It enhances the productivity, the effectiveness, and the quality of the other factors of production' (ibid. p. 61), and so adds value by increasing the values of other resources: 'Hence, the measurement of the value of content will be possible only through some type of aggregate analysis and not with traditional productivity equations' (ibid.).

Repo (1989) gives a thorough and considered review of research by economists, accounting researchers and management scientists on the economics of information. With few exceptions the work reported has been theoretical rather than empirical[3] and heavily influenced by the concept of reducing uncertainty. The encounters of economists with information theory seem to have been fairly disastrous; as Repo points out, almost all the theoretical studies have been influenced by Shannon, with only a few taking a cognitive approach.

Repo also makes a clear distinction between information and information product, 'though it is seldom made by economists', few of whom have made the other important distinction between products and services either (Repo, 1989, p. 73). Similarly, 'Classical economists, and even many modern economists, do not make the distinction between exchange and use' (ibid). The cognitive approach – not much used by the researchers cited by Repo – is also criticized by him for failing to pay heed to information as product, while doing justice to its role in communication.

He concludes that:

> economic approaches based on 'information theory' have not achieved significant practical results in a general sense, but 'classical' economic approaches can and should be used in describing information products (and services) in terms of exchange values ... [while] the cognitive approach, with analysis of the tasks performed, should be used simultaneously for describing the value-in-use of information (ibid. p. 68).

He also considers that the statistical approach is appropriate in stable, predictable areas, while the cognitive mode is more useful in 'changing situations'. His final words are in favour of the value-in-use approach:

> It is apparent that information as a product will be under extensive research due to economic pressures on information activities. It is also inevitable that it is not possible to explain fully the value of information in terms of exchange values. The key point in assessing value is in the use of information (ibid. p. 83).

'Information economics'

In recent years the concept of a specific economics of information has been promoted (see, for example, Parker et al., 1988). While the emphasis is on making value decisions on IT investment, the thinking is equally applicable to resources of information itself and of knowledge.

The basic point of the argument for information economics is that cost-benefit analysis is no longer an adequate tool for evaluating applications that are innovative or that produce/enhance revenue, nor yet for justifying the long-term investment necessary for developing information infrastructures. Traditional cost-benefit analysis, based on easily measurable and tangible benefits 'presents a limited view of the costs and benefits of information availability within the enterprise'; the new information economics 'must assess benefits not previously thought to be quantifiable' and 'the quantification must be demonstrable to be accepted by executives in the business domain and the CEO' (Parker et al., 1989, p. 233).

Additions to traditional cost-benefit analysis proposed by Parker et al. include:

- *value linking and value acceleration analysis*: to assess costs that enable benefits to be received elsewhere in the organization – via a ripple effect or by causing benefits to be received more quickly;
- *value restructuring analysis*: used in estimating effects of modifying job functions – as in moving to higher value activities and so increasing the contribution of those carrying out the activities, e.g. R&D, legal, personnel departments; a useful technique when there is no direct link to bottom line performance;
- *innovative evaluation*: for evaluating and choosing among new and untried alternatives (predictive investment evaluation); it sets the competitive value of innovation against the risk involved.

Parker and her co-authors also propose a shift from the concept of benefits to that of values, and introduce new classes of value, which provide 'appropriate methods to assess the importance of benefits previously classed as intangible', going beyond simple return-on-investment calculations:

- *enhanced return on investment*: employing the cost-benefit enhancements mentioned above;
- *strategic match*: assessing the degree to which proposed IT projects support corporate strategic goals;
- *competitive advantage*;
- *management information*: assessing the contribution to management's need for information on core activities of the business;
- *competitive response*: assessment of the degree of corporate risk associated with *not* undertaking projects.

Wiseman (1992) reports on practical applications of the Parker approach: one such application involved bringing together business 'units' in a UK government department with the central IT management group; another was concerned with evaluation of a management information system. She stresses in both cases the strength of the approach in helping communication between IT professionals and business managers in assessing organizational risk factors.

WHY SHOULD BUSINESSES TRY TO VALUE INFORMATION ANYWAY?

It is a commonplace today to speak of information as a potentially profitable resource, and so it is indeed. But without a policy that compels attention to the nature and extent of the resource, how it is used, and how it contributes to corporate objectives, the potential will be unrealized and loss rather than profit will be the likely outcome. (Orna, 1990, p. 18)

In the years since these words were written, the idea that organizations need strategies for information that are aligned with their business strategies has perhaps found greater acceptance. But unless businesses can assign a reliable value to their information resources and to the results of applying them, one that has equal standing with money values, the idea is unlikely to become a reality, because it cannot carry conviction with the decision-makers.

This in itself brings dangers. Failure to define what constitutes the essential information food for the organisational knowledge base can lead to:

- 'savings' by 'outsourcing'; or 'downsizing'; which actually destroy resources which are a potential liferaft rather than superfluous deck cargo;
- missed opportunities of bringing together relevant information from different sources to bear on urgent problems, or to create new products (ironic at a time when 'data warehousing' is being promoted as a means of doing this);
- failure to spot potential threats in time because of lack of intelligence gathering and correlation;
- failure in attempts to innovate;
- persistence in inappropriate and wasteful information activities, and failure to recognize opportunities for using information resources more productively.

SOME APPROACHES TO THE PROCESS

While finding sound and rigorous ways of valuing information has not been an over-tilled field of research, it certainly has not been neglected, and it is encouraging that in the last few years there has been an increasing number of serious and respectable studies. And these are perhaps more likely to be well received from the accounting side nowadays – in the related context of human factors and organization design, the Advisory Committee on Science and Technology recently pointed out that the objection to action that cannot be shown directly to enhance the 'bottom line' is 'being undermined as accountancy principles embrace the need to value "intangibles" ' (ACOST 1993).

The approaches are essentially of two kinds: the 'direct attack', and what might be termed taking the problem obliquely from the flank.

Direct attack

Koenig (1992) surveys work from a variety of sources in the US which has attempted to 'value and evaluate the effect of providing information services', starting with work in the 1970s, at the Exxon Research Center and in NASA among others, which looked at data about the use and impact of in-house information products and services, and which attempted to calculate a cost-benefit ratio on the basis of the reports of researchers using the information services. In all cases the benefits – calculated on quite rigorous bases – exceeded the costs by factors ranging from 11:1 to 2:1.

Methodologies of this general type have been most fully developed and widely applied by King Research, Inc. (again in the US), and Koenig outlines the results of their studies in government agencies and in private corporations. The method developed by King Research analyses:

1   the value of information services to the organization in terms of the value of the time (measured by salary and overhead) that users are willing to expend on them;
2   the additional costs that would be incurred if there were no in-house information service and information had to be acquired from elsewhere;
3   the savings that would be lost and the research costs that would be incurred if there were no in-house information service.

On each of these measures the benefits consistently exceed the costs. Koenig also cites a striking calculation by Griffiths and King (1988) over a range of their studies, for the value of reading various kinds of information products:

For reading a journal article	$385
For reading a book	$1160
For reading an internal technical document	$706

While acknowledging that calculating cost-benefit figures is a 'complex and disputatious exercise', especially where it concerns information, Koenig points out that there is still a striking magnitude and consistency of effects reported 'both across different techniques and across different cases' (Koenig, 1992, p. 203). The significance of these measures is that they show clearly positive benefits from the most heavily attacked way of providing information – the in-house information centre or service. They do not look at the other information resources – internal and external – used by organizations, which are often not recognized as information, and whose value is, by virtue of that, perhaps more likely to be recognized.

Broadbent and Lofgren also report on applications of a form of cost-benefit analysis for evaluating library and information services. Their approach, which draws on that of Griffiths and King, allows assignment of costs and benefits in money equivalent terms, and they report that it 'consistently identified very positive cost-benefit ratios' (Broadbent and Lofgren, 1993, p. 697). They emphasize the importance of 'measuring the outputs and outcomes that key stake-holders regard as important' (ibid. p. 699).

The oblique approach

A more widespread approach to valuing information is through seeking indirect evidence of its value to businesses in promoting competitiveness, productivity, or innovation and successful marketing of the results. A recent book on *The Value of Information to the Intelligent Organisation* (Abell, 1994) exemplifies this approach; its themes include case-study evidence of the benefits of: organizational structures that make the most of human skills and knowledge, 'empowerment' of employees, openness of the 'company knowledge base', bringing together information from a range of sources, using IT to draw on global 'digital information fields', and adding value to information by presenting it in forms that customers can use direct.

Nor is there any shortage of research which indicates strongly that getting appropriate information and using it in these ways actually brings advantages in terms of competitiveness, productivity and innovation.

Competitiveness

Many of the ideas involved here derive from Porter's concept of the 'value chain' (see for example, Porter and Miller, 1985) – the series of interdependent 'value activities' in which businesses engage and the 'linkages' which connect them. While the emphasis is on the use of IT to achieve competitive advantage by delivering cheaper or more highly differentiated products and services, it 'must be conceived of broadly to encompass the information that businesses create and use' as well as the technologies used for processing information. So the technology can help to capture, enhance and organize the information associated with value activities and increase the company's ability to get more out of linkages and flows of information.

A particularly interesting study in this field comes from Bowonder and Miyake, who summarize a range of research findings on information management and competitiveness, and also present the results of their own research in Nippon Steel Corporation in Japan. The research findings they cite indicate that the strategic use of information systems and IT facilitates competitiveness in a number of ways:

- productivity improvements via quality inspection and control;
- better control and optimization;
- quick information exchange;
- large-scale storage of information;
- understanding of market dynamics;
- stimulation of IT business or activities in the firm;
- strategy to jump ahead of rivals through 'better anticipatory, forward-looking scanning systems' (Bowander and Miyake, 1992, p. 42).

On the basis of their own research, they identify the specific strategies that have helped Nippon Steel Corporation to become and remain competitive:

- horizontal as opposed to vertical information flow structures and management controls;
- the maintenance of a large centralized database at company headquarters networked to various units;
- 'continuous and regular environmental scanning or technology monitoring' (ibid. p. 43);
- technology fusion - by the combination of various technologies;
- globalization and strategic alliances with other companies;
- 'organizational learning by which an enterprise is able to observe, assess and act upon stimuli which are either internal or external to the organization in cumulative, interactive and purposeful ways' (ibid. p. 43);

- strategic information systems at corporate level;
- intensive skill development in the use of information-systems and IT strategies.

Their conclusion is that Nippon Steel has used

> ... a combination of information management strategies for:
>
> - sustaining competitiveness in existing business segments (steel);
> - creating competitiveness by developing new business segments (IT);
> - continuously creating new information technology-related equipment/ machinery for various segments (IT); and
> - conceptualizing, developing, implementing and networking management information systems (MIS) and developing competence in emerging technological areas. (ibid. p. 54)

Risk avoidance/reduction of uncertainty

The factors of risk avoidance and reduction of uncertainty are often coupled together in discussions of the value of information, but it is perhaps more useful to unhitch them and to look at them separately.

As we have seen (p. 23), many economists have been hung up on information theory and its emphasis on reducing uncertainty – without paying much regard to the fact that the main concern of those who developed that theory was with the transmission of messages, rather than their information content. Risk avoidance is another matter, and there is a real sense in which information as defined in this chapter can help businesses to make appropriate strategic choices in hazardous situations, and to spot 'icebergs' while there's still time to get out of the way.

The points made by Bowonder and Miyake about the value of environmental scanning and technology monitoring, and organizational learning (see p. 27) are relevant to the identification of potential external risks while they are still on the horizon. There is also evidence that the free flow of information within businesses is a positive factor in successful management of the risks of turbulent times. Olson (1977) found that, in science-based firms, management philosophies which isolated key groups of workers and discouraged openness and the transfer of information led to them becoming less able to meet their objectives; and Rothwell concluded from his studies of successes and failures in innovation that 'Maximising information reduces uncertainty and risks' (Rothwell, 1984, p. 9). Peters writing for US businesses in a period of what he describes as 'generic uncertainty' (Peters, 1988, p. 36) prescribes openness and information sharing as one of the essentials of survival.

Productivity

Koenig also looks at 'indirect' evidence of the value of information, in the form of studies of the characteristics of productive companies, in which 'a very consistent thread is the importance of information access and information services' (Koenig, 1992, p. 203). For example, in electronics/instrumentation firms the key differentiator between more and less productive organizations – measured by rates of growth and return on assets – was found to be information-valuing behaviour on the part of managers, in terms of encouraging use of information, publication, visits, etc.

Koenig's own studies in the pharmaceutical industry – based on the number of approved new drugs per research dollar expended – revealed differences in the information environment of more and less productive firms. The more productive show:

- greater openness to outside information;
- less concern with protecting proprietary information;
- greater information systems development effort;
- greater end-user use of information systems and more encouragement of browsing and serendipity;
- greater technical and subject sophistication of information services staff.

Innovation

Koenig links his findings about productivity with the body of literature 'that finds that contact with external information sources and diversity of information sources are key factors in successful innovation' (1992, p. 205). That literature is well epitomized by Bowden and Ricketts (1992) in one of the last NEDO publications before its demise, and by such studies as those of Fransman (1992) and Newby (1993). (Much of the text in this section is based on Orna (1993) with acknowledgements to Aslib for permission to quote.)

Among the points relevant to the value of information are these:

- R&D investment is a necessary but not a sufficient condition for successful innovation. Successful innovative firms keep a close eye on the market, and on demographic and social change; and they spend a lot of time listening to their customers.
- R&D is a 'capital stock of knowledge which can be built up over time but which depreciates' (Bowden and Ricketts, 1992, pp. 30-1) – so it needs feeding and maintaining by constant new inputs of information. And the maintenance depends on 'managerial and organizational skills to apply' the inputs of information (Newby, 1993, [5]).
- A well educated and skilled labour force helps innovation because 'it makes it easier to introduce new technology successfully and to develop techniques by drawing upon workers' informal knowledge and experience' (Bowden and Ricketts, 1992, p. 44) and it increases the pool from which new ideas can come.
- Risk in innovation is minimized by:
  - being able to draw on internally generated information;
  - close associations between buyers and suppliers;
  - good communications between upstream and downstream operations;
  - high trust between the parties involved, including shareholders.
- The chances of success are reduced by:

- – concentration on expensive high-technology projects to the exclusion of diffusion-oriented policies which emphasize knowledge, standards and training;
  - – 'short-termism' in funding and commitment, and in managerial incentives – because 'Innovative activities imply costs today and returns in the future' (Bowden and Ricketts, 1992, p. 73).
- Success in working towards and implementing innovation is supported by:
  - – people from different functions working together in teams;
  - – good communications inside firms and between them and outside;
  - – clear lines of communication and free sharing of information;
  - – informal information structures.
- Success in competition depends on:
  - – understanding other companies, competitors, collaborators and suppliers;
  - – understanding the changing relationships between competitors and collaborators;
  - – information exchange and good lines of communication between professionals from the same discipline who are employed in different businesses;
  - – knowing what information should be kept within the company and what can with benefit be shared: 'What one keeps to oneself and what one shares is ... the essence of management of competition' (Bower, 1992, p. 26).
- The key assets of successful businesses are those 'associated with knowledge and its accumulation' (Bowden and Ricketts, 1992, p. 220).
- The most useful contributions to success in innovation and competition that governments can make are:
  - – investment in education and training;
  - – supporting and complementing the knowledge of individual businesses by collecting, storing and spreading information from a wide range of fields that have a bearing on their activities (see for example Fransman's account of the Japanese innovation system);
  - – developing an effective network for spreading information between industry and academic research.

Bawden contributes another strand to this discussion, with his study of how an 'information-rich environment' (Bawden, 1986, p. 214) at the organizational level contributes to the creativity which is one of the motors that drives innovation.

But how much ice does the evidence cut?

But, for all this evidence of the value of information to businesses, we still have to remember that, as Ducker warns us, it cuts little ice with most senior executives. He goes through the arguments for investment in information – especially about the external environment in which companies operate – and discounts their effectiveness one by one:

1   Cost saving? 'The efficiency argument is rarely used in relation to the per-
    formance of the most expensive people ... they do not perceive that their
    performance could be measured in terms of efficiency' (Ducker, 1991, p. 5).
2   Risk assessment? They find it difficult to accept that 'their judgement may
    be based on an inadequate awareness of the environment, that they can
    minimize risk by continuously improving and maintaining their awareness'
    (ibid. p. 26).
3   Substitution cost? 'This argument is largely vitiated because few senior
    executives have any idea what it costs to get information' (ibid. p. 26).
4   Maximizing revenue opportunity? An easy argument to demonstrate for
    basic information such as mailing lists; much more difficult to deploy
    when you are 'trying to persuade them that improving their awareness of
    their environment might lead them to identify trends in the markets or in
    technology and hence initiate research and development projects which
    could lead to new products' (except in the pharmaceutical industry)
    (ibid. p. 27).

CONTEMPORARY METHODOLOGIES FOR VALUING INFORMATION

What has been said so far may well suggest that putting a reliable and acceptable value to information is a mighty difficult task, and that, while there is
plenty of indirect evidence to suggest it has a positive value to those who
know how to use it, no one has found a direct method applicable across a wide
range of situations. But, fortunately, that isn't exactly the case; in recent years
there have been significant developments in methodology, supported by spe-
cially designed software which are described below.

The technology

Infomapper

First in the field were Burk and Horton (1988). Their Infomapper software is
designed to help organizations to get an overview of their information
resources, not just to assign a value to them. Widely used since its introduction, particularly in the US, it has recently been criticized – Barclay and
Oppenheim (1994) – as too slow and too US-biased for general application. The
criticisms have, however, been countered by Horton. Defending the 'first
product of its kind in the marketplace' (Horton, 1994, p. 120), he indicates that
the developers plan to add new features in the next standalone release.

   One of the points that Horton makes in reply to the criticism referred to
above is the time needed to plan and carry through an information resources
inventory (Horton's own recommended minimum time for this sort of study
is six months), and the human resources required for the task. (For a con-
sideration of the human contribution to the use of this kind of software, see
p. 33.)

Audit-tracking of information use

Woods, writing specifically about marketing information, has referred to software which enables 'the audit tracking of specific parcels of information to become a reality' (Woods, 1992, p. 362) and so to 'see where information has come from, where it has been and where it ends up' and to relate the use of information to the achievement of objectives. This should contribute to what he calls 'externalization' – the stage where the value given to information internally 'having been measured and improved upon, is now sufficiently well documented that it can be compared with external standards to ascertain its market value' (ibid. p. 363).

Total value methodology (TVM)

McPherson has developed applications software specifically directed towards integrating 'intangible' values of information with more tangible values, so as to achieve 'a treatment of intangible value that is so rigorous that it has to be accepted as an equal partner to monetary value' (McPherson, 1994a, p. 203). In order to make those corporate benefits from strategic and organizational objectives which are supported directly by 'informational activity' explicit (ibid. p. 208) a new value dimension is needed that can be put on equal terms alongside economic value added to give 'combined value added' (ibid.).

He distinguishes (McPherson, 1994b) seven types of value contribution to the outputs of a business:

1 *Business value*: owner or shareholder value.
2 *Internal value*: the value of knowledge, know-how and information contained within the business, and the ability to deploy these attributes to provide useful effort via organization and information systems.
3 *Non-physical asset value*: 'Intangible Fixed Assets', e.g. brands, patents, intellectual property, publishing rights.
4 *Operational output value*: instrumental value of commercial operations – typically measured as Net Cash Flow and leading to 'bottom-line' value deriving from the Profit and Loss Account and Funds Flow Account of financial statements.
5 *Transfer to customer*: the value transferred to customers by means of goods and services received and paid for; more than just the cash value, it covers also the value to customers of the price they pay.
6 *Fixed asset value*: the intrinsic value of fixed assets.
7 *Environmental impact*: on the 'natural, social and moral' environments.

McPherson's methodology is based on the 'axiological' concepts mentioned earlier (see pp. 19 and 38), in that it provides a structured framework that is logical in itself, but independent of the inputs of subjective human perspectives (for more about them, see below). It draws intellectual strength and rigour from disciplines not usually tapped by those who have concerned themselves with the value of information – primarily in systems engineering, and also axiology, decision theory and measurement theory.

The TVM interactive computer aid which McPherson has designed permits defining 'a proper logical space in which a set of combinatorial rules express the meaning and consequent quantity of combined value, given the definition of the inputs' (McPherson, 1994a, p. 212). It generates simple visualizations which display the combination of aggregate monetary value and aggregate intangible value brought together in a three-dimensional space. The visualizations are said to 'be very effective in helping evaluators obtain an understanding of the implications of value combinations' (ibid. p. 213).

The author claims for the methodology that it leads to better understanding of the relationship between intangible and monetary value; reliable comparisons between the overall performance of alternative information assets; confidence in the 'quasi-objectivity of the results'; and better cost justification and investment decisions. (ibid. p. 214).

The human contribution

Like all good methods, those just described entail a combination of human and technological inputs, and their authors emphasize that the quality of the outputs depends on human thinking – thinking devoted to establishing appropriate criteria, agreeing on what key business objectives mean and defining information in terms of the individual organization (in other words, getting what Drucker (1994) calls 'the theory of the business' into good shape).

Burk and Horton (1988) define the essential human contribution as identifying 'elements of value' of 'information resource entities'.[4] For example:

- the quality of information itself (e.g. accuracy, comprehensiveness, currency, reliability);
- the utility of information holdings (e.g. accessibility, ease of use);
- impact on organizational productivity (e.g. improved decision-making, time-saving, improvement in product quality);
- impact on organizational effectiveness (e.g. finding new markets, improved customer satisfaction, product differentiation);
- impact on financial position (e.g. cost reduction or saving, improved profits, return on investment) (Burk and Horton, 1988, pp. 92–7).

Human thinking is indispensable too in ranking information resource entities in terms of their overall value to the organization. The software depends on human knowledge of the organization, and human judgement for inputs that will yields valid rankings.

Application of McPherson's methodology also depends on human value judgements: 'human perceptions on preferences and utilities are needed to "tune" certain variable parameters ... [on setting up the software] ... so that the embodied criterion reflects the value set as articulated by senior management' (McPherson, 1994a, p. 213). A series of 'subjective' human assessments is essential for 'feeding' the software so that it can apply the combinatorial rules built into it: value inputs at the bottom level; judgements of the contribution made to the next higher goal by increments in individual utilities; assignment of weights – the relative importance of individual values to the next *33* higher goal (McPherson, 1994b, p. 29). These judgements have to go back to organizational objectives and the mission statement, and they demand not only hard individual thinking at levels of disaggregation not often approached in organizations, but also negotiation, discussion and resolution of contradictions by a group of people. It is small wonder that the methodology requires a 'facilitator' to mediate and interpret between the evaluators and the software.

The emphasis of the methodology is on situations where change is contemplated, and where it can be used for exploration or monitoring rather than as an absolute measure. Applications to date have been primarily in organizations which have been prepared to make the necessary investment of thinking time; they include a telecommunications company seeking to evaluate a proposed new information system development, and a governmental organization in the process of developing an information-technology strategy which depends on identifying the value of information as a national resource.

CURRENT OPPORTUNITIES FOR ESTABLISHING THE VALUE OF INFORMATION

The title of this chapter implies an undertaking to look at 'problems and opportunities' in valuing information, and the evidence so far presented suggests that both exist in abundance. It is now time to evaluate what the opportunities are and the problems that prevent businesses from taking advantage of them.

It can certainly be said that it is now feasible, as well as desirable, to assign a reliable and respectable value to information . Given the emphasis in the available methodologies and in the research studies on the organization as a total system, and on the significance of strategic objectives, it seems sensible to place attempts to assign value to information within the framework of some organization-wide change process. Two possible contexts are business process re-engineering and the development of organizational informal policy.

In the context of Business Process Re-engineering

The methodologies now available can be applied within the currently popular framework of Business Process Re-engineering (or Business Process Redesign, or Process Innovation – to name but a handful of the variants). Indeed it makes the success of these approaches much more likely because information links human and technological resources and, as we have seen (see p. 20), enters into all business processes.

Davenport (1993) gives a particularly clear and convincing exposition of the relationship between processes and information. In introducing it, he makes the useful point that 'much information in organisations and processes – more than 85%, by some estimates – is not manipulated by information technology' (p. 71). He also observes sharply that

> ... despite much talk and writing about the 'Information Age', few organisations
> have treated information management as a domain worthy of serious improve-
> ment efforts. Progress in managing information is rarely described or measured;

providers of less-structured information in organisations (eg libraries, competitive analysis functions, and market research groups) often have relatively low status and confused reporting relationships; vast amounts of information enter and leave organisations without anyone's being fully aware of their impact, value, or cost. (p. 72)

He describes the potential roles of information in the whole range of business processes:

- *Process performance monitoring*: advantage goes to those businesses that are effective in managing and monitoring information about quality;
- *Process integration*: information is the 'glue' that holds an organizational structure together;
- *Process customisation*: information about a firm's customers can be managed to allow tailoring of products and services;
- *Information-oriented management processes*: 'most firms concentrate on financial information generated from accounting systems, which, as has been widely recognized, is frequently misleading or useless for management purposes' – what really needs managing in order to assist these processes is unstructured and externally generated information, and that needs human analytical skills combined with sophisticated technology;
- *Information-oriented operational processes*: information and information products are more and more often the primary outputs of businesses, but the activities involved 'are unlikely to have been viewed and managed as processes' (p. 82).

Davenport advocates a new approach to the management of information in a process context. For a start, the traditional assumption that information acquisition, analysis and distribution 'is work better managed by subordinates' (p. 86), needs to be ditched. Then the lumping together of IT and information content needs to be dissolved – especially now that a reaction which has set in against the overselling of IT tends to bring information itself into discredit. Functions, such as corporate libraries and information centres, which handle unstructured or external information must be rescued from their isolation from 'anything strategic or operationally critical' and brought close to key management processes, such as strategy planning (he cites the examples of 'competitive information centers' in Japan (p. 87).

Finally he cautions against the application of concept of 'information engineering', with its models of data elements and relationships, and its rigorous approach to separating applications from data, to information-oriented processes. For instance, the document might more profitably be considered as the primary unit of information analysis, rather than the data elements that make up documents. The future may, indeed, lie with combining object orientation and process thinking; this will require agreement on 'the meaning and usage of information entities', and wide and free sharing of information across functions and units (an unlikely prospect, he admits, because of the prevalence of 'information politics') (p. 90).

In the context of developing organizational information policy and strategy

The methods described here for assigning value to information also fit well into the context of developing organizational information policies. An organizational information policy is described by Orna (1990, p. 19) as being based on the organization's key objectives, and as defining:

- the objectives of using information in relation to corporate objectives;
- the resources of information and the resources for managing it which the organization needs in order to achieve its objectives;
- the people who manage information and their responsibilities;
- the systems and technology for managing information to support people in achieving their objectives;
- criteria for assessing the costs and benefits of information to the organization;
- criteria for monitoring and evaluating information activities.

Such policies don't have much chance of acceptance and implementation unless they seriously address criteria for the costs and values of information.

The approach also fits within Drucker's (1994) formulation of 'the theory of the business' – that is, the assumptions which a business makes about:

1 its environment: society and its structure, the market, the customer, technology;
2 its mission;
3 the core competencies it needs to accomplish its mission.

The theory must be 'known and understood throughout the organization' and it has to be tested constantly. 'It is not graven on tablets of stone. It is a hypothesis. And it is a hypothesis about things that are in constant flux' (p. 101). So a successful theory must be based on information that feeds the right kind of knowledge and helps knowledge to keep pace with change, and on thinking.

PROBLEMS THAT COULD PREVENT THE OPPORTUNITIES BEING TAKEN

While it is now feasible, for the first time, to set a reliable value on the most important kinds of information that organizations need to feed their knowledge, the very merits of what is on offer bring problems in their train.

First, the good news may not spread very rapidly because, quite understandably, organizations which have carried out successful evaluations may well not wish to talk about them in detail.

Second, getting the goods isn't just a matter of buying a black box. The methods now available, as their originators emphasize, depend heavily on human thinking at all levels from the most detailed to the strategic –

and spending time on taking thought is little favoured in economies suffering what Hutton (1994) describes as the 'curse of the Anglo-Saxons': that of being in thrall to short-term payback. On the other hand, however, thinking may be due to return to favour as a low-risk and cost-effective investment, in the wake of the disillusionments brought about by large investments in IT systems made without those responsible, in Davies' words (Abell, 1994), 'analysing what they wish to get out of them' and getting just about what they deserved.

The methods also require value judgements related to strategic objectives, and it has to be said, alas, that the quality of human value judgements in this context cannot be taken for granted; there is plenty of evidence that senior managers in a business do not necessarily even share a common view of what their organization's mission statement and objective mean (see, for example, Wilson, 1984).

Finally, any business going into this area needs to be aware of the realities of organizational change and information politics, for they will certainly come to the fore and the way they are handled will determine the outcome.

> Unless the politics of information are identified and managed, companies will not move into the Information Age. Information will not be shared freely nor used effectively by decision makers. No amount of data modeling, no number of relational databases, and no invocation of the 'information-based organization' will bring about a new political order of information. Rather, it will take what politics always take: negotiation, influence-exercising, back-room deals, coalition-building, and occasionally even war. If information is truly to become the most valued commodity in the business of the future, we cannot expect to acquire it without an occasional struggle.' (Davenport *et al.*, 1992, pp. 64–65).

If information and knowledge resources can be reliably valued, if a business commits itself to the endeavour to value them and to acting on the results, and if they turn out to be a great deal more valuable than had been assumed, then the world of organisational values could be turned upside down. The assumption quoted by Davenport (see page 35) that the work of information management is something for subordinates would be challenged, and there could well be either a hostile reaction from those who have held it, or even attempts to take over these hitherto despised territories by those ambitious for advancement.

Organizations which seriously want to take advantage of the opportunities that now exist for establishing the value of their resources of information and knowledge must be prepared to devote time to thinking, and to bring all the key stakeholders together to express their own judgement and reach agreement on the inputs that will determine the values which will emerge. In that process they should be prepared to give due weight to the knowledge of that group of stakeholders constituted by professional information managers. For some organizations, this might be a novel prescription but, if it is not followed, the chances of success will be proportionately limited.

NOTES

1   Readers who are interested in exploring the neglected domain of axiology will find much to reflect on in Hartman (1967). He distinguishes between two modes of knowing – 'the natural and the valuational', knowledge about things and their attributes, and a higher order knowledge which embraces the value of things: 'The valuational ... does not refer to the individual thing ... but to the concept, or rather to [the thing] as possessing the properties of this concept: a thing is good if it fulfils the intention of its concept' (p. 103).

2   The information–knowledge distinction: knowledge is inside our heads, what we have learned from experience of the world and what we use to guide our actions. Information is outside in the world – in various forms, print on paper, electronic, spoken, etc. We have to transform information into knowledge before we can make use of it. We also engage in the complementary process of transforming our knowledge into information and putting it outside in the world in order to communicate it to others (see Orna and Stevens, 1991, 1993).

3   Koenig (1990) remarks 'What is striking about the literature is the ratio, at least six to one, between articles that discuss either the difficulty of arriving at any quantifiable data or the difficulty of discussing methodology abstractly ..., and articles that actually apply a methodology and develop some data. The ratio is presumably a function of both the importance of the topic and of the difficulty of addressing if satisfactorily.'

4   Information Resource Entity: 'a configuration of people, things, energy, information and other inputs that has the capacity to create, acquire, provide, process, store or disseminate information (Burk and Horton, 1988, p. 21) and that can be managed as a resource. Examples: libraries and information centres: management information systems: publishing services.

REFERENCES

Abell, A. (1993), 'Business Link Hertfordshire', *Business Information Review,* **10** (2), pp. 48–55.

Abell, A. (ed.) (1994), *The Value of Information to the Intelligent Organisation,* Hatfield; University of Hertfordshire Press.

ACOST (Advisory Council on Science and Technology) (1993), *People, Technology and Organisations. The Application of Human Factors and Organisational Design,* Cabinet Office (Office of Public Service and Science) & Advisory Council on Science and Technology, London: HMSO.

Akeroyd, J. (1991), 'Costing and Pricing Information: The Bottom Line', *Aslib Proceedings,* **43** (2/3), pp. 87–92.

Barclay, K. and Oppenheim, D. (1994), 'An Evaluation of InfoMapper Software at Trainload Coal', *Aslib Proceedings,* **46** (2), pp. 31–42.

Bawden, D. (1986), 'Information Systems and the Stimulation of Creativity', *Journal of Information Science,* **12,** pp. 203–16.

Bowden, A. and Ricketts, M. (eds) (1992), *Stimulating Innovation in Industry. The Challenge for the United Kingdom*, London: Kogan Page/NEDO.

Bower, J.L. (1992), *The Organization of Markets*, Harvard Business School, Division of Research. Working Paper 92–032.

Bowonder, B. and Miyake, T. (1992), 'Creating and Sustaining Competitiveness: Information Management Strategies of Nippon Steel Corporation', *International Journal of Information Management*, **12**, pp. 39–56.

Broadbent, M. and Lofgren, H. (1993), 'Information Delivery: Identifying Priorities, Performance, and Value', *Information Processing and Management*, **29** (6), pp. 683–701.

Brookes, B. C. (1980), 'Informatics as the Fundamental Social Science', in P. Taylor (ed.), *New Trends in Documentation and Information*. Proceedings of the 39th FID Congress. London: Aslib.

Burk, C.F. Jr and Horton, F.W. (1988), *Infomap: A Complete Guide to Discovering Corporate Information Resources*, Englewood Cliffs, NJ: Prentice Hall.

Davenport, T.H. et al. (1992), 'Information Politics', *Sloan Management Review*, Fall, pp. 53–65.

Davenport, T.H. (1993), *Process Innovation. Reengineering Work through Information Technology*, Boston, MA: Harvard Business School Press.

Drucker, P.F. (1994), 'The Theory of the Business', *Harvard Business Review*, September–October, pp. 95–104.

Ducker, J. (1991), 'Information and the Getting of Wisdom', *The Intelligent Enterprise*, **1** (9/10), pp. 24–7.

Fransman, M. (1992), 'The Japanese Innovation System: How it Works', *Science in Parliament*, **49** (4), pp. 25–30.

Griffiths, J-M. and King, D.W. (1988), *An Information Audit of Public Service Electric and Gas Company Libraries and Information Resources: Executive Summary and Conclusions*, Rockville, MD: King Research Inc., 15pp.

Hartman, R.W. (1967), *The Structure of Value: Foundations of Scientific Axiology*, London & Amsterdam: Southern Illinois University Press, Feffer & Simons Inc.

Horton, F.W. Jr (1994), 'InfoMapper Revisited', *Aslib Proceedings*, **46** (4), pp. 117–20.

Hutton, W. (1994), 'Curse of the Anglo-Saxons', *The Guardian,* 26 September.

Ingwersen, P. (1992), 'Information and Information Science in Context', *Libri*, **42** (3), pp. 99–135.

Johannessen, J.A. and Olaisen, J. (1993), 'Information, Communication and Innovation: Identifying Critical Innovation Factors (CIF)', *Information Management and Computer Security*, **1** (4), pp. 29–36.

Koenig, M. (1992), 'The Importance of Information Services for Productivity "Under-recognized" and Under-invested', *Special Libraries*, Fall, pp. 199–210.

Machlup, F. (1979), 'Uses, Value, and Benefits of Knowledge', *Knowledge: Creation, Diffusion, Utilization*, **1** (1), pp. 62–81. (Reproduced in D.W. King, et al. (eds), *Key Papers in the Economics of Information*, New York: American Society of Information Science/Knowledge Industry Publications Inc. 1989.)

McPherson, P. K. (1991), *Note on the Axiological Basis of the SWAP Evaluation*

Framework, Kenninghall, Norwich: The MacPherson Consultancy.

McPherson, P. K. (1994a), 'Accounting for the Value of Information', *Aslib Proceedings*, **46** (9), pp. 203–215.

McPherson, P. K. (1994b), *The Systems Engineering of Business Value. An Introductory Notebook. Version 2.2*, Kenninghall, Norwich: The MacPherson Consultancy.

Newby, H. (1993), *Innovation and the Social Sciences: The Way Ahead*, Swindon: Economic and Social Research Council.

Olson, E. E. (1977), 'Organizational Factors Affecting Information Flow in Industry', *Aslib Proceedings*, **29** (1), pp. 2–11.

Orna, E. (1990), *Practical Information Policies. How to Manage Information Flow in Organizations*, Aldershot: Gower.

Orna, E. (1993), 'Full, Co-operative, and Profitable Use of China's Information Resources – Foundations for a Policy', *Aslib Proceedings*, **45** (10), pp. 257–9.

Parker, M. M., Benson, R. J. and Trainer, H. E. (1988), *Information Economics: Linking Business Performance to Information Technology*, Englewood Cliffs, NJ: Prentice Hall.

Porter, M. E. and Miller, V. E. (1985), 'How Information Gives you Competitive Advantages', *Harvard Business Review*, July–August, pp. 149–60.

Repo, A. J. (1989), 'The Value of Information: Approaches in Economics, Accounting, and Management Science', *JASIS*, **40** (2), pp. 68–85.

Wilson, B. (1984), *Systems: Concepts, Methodologies, and Applications*, London: John Wiley.

Rothwell, R. (1984), 'Information and Successful Innovation', in *Information for Industry: the Next Ten Years BL R&D Report 5802*, London: BL R&D Technical Change Centre.

Wiseman, D. (1992), 'Information Economics: A Practical Approach to Valuing Information Systems', *Journal of Information Technology,* **7**, pp. 169–76.

Woods, B. (1992), 'The Evaluation of Marketing Information: Some Current Practices and Trends', *Aslib Proceedings*, **44** (10), pp. 361–4.

ACKNOWLEDGEMENTS

I am indebted to Professor P.K. McPherson for helpful discussions and comments.

3 Resolving the imbalance between information and technology

Clive Holtham

Following on from the topics raised in the last chapter, Clive Holtham, in this wide-ranging paper, argues for the need for clarity of terms, usage and practice and for clarity in the way we discuss information. He propounds the need for a new paradigm in the management of the resource itself rather than upon the management of the technology.

After a brief analysis as to why this is necessary he discusses the characteristics of hard and soft data, considers the key skills needed in the areas of 'Informating', and review the disciplines which are now contributing to the emergence of a unified discipline of information management. He argues for the emergence of an NIP, the new information professional, to take its place beside the established business disciplines such as marketing and accounting (see also Bill Cook in Chapter 6)

Holtham concludes that only change brought about by crisis will be of sufficient scale to bring about the required shift in perceptions and in corporate attention.

Information is more critical to business success than information technology (IT), but IT gets most of the attention and the great bulk of the investment in managerial time, financial investment, and media attention. It is argued here that the continuation of this imbalance will be at the heart of failure to achieve the full benefits from business information systems. Yet for several reasons it will be difficult to overcome the imbalance. One approach is to develop the concept of the 'new information professional'.

DEFINITIONAL PROBLEMS, AND THE URGENT NEED FOR CLARIFICATION

There is a lack of any generally accepted definition of information or even of IT. This is a problem in both academic and business terms. Yet the need for greater clarity and insight in this area is ever-increasing because of:

1 the growth of 'multimedia', spanning the boundaries of historically diverse disciplines;
2 the suggested inevitability of an 'Information Superhighway';
3 the creation of technologies such as 'virtual reality' whose proponents argue can have a profound impact on personal and business life;
4 the need for a new paradigm as computers in business generally begin to move beyond the confines of formal, structured 'hard' data processing (DP) into the sharing and exchange of informal and unstructured 'soft' data.

The paradigms of first generation computing (1949–present) are very heavily geared to 'hard' data organized on a functional basis (traditional DP) or on a personal basis (traditional personal computing). A move to a paradigm of information management need not reject the hard-won benefits of traditional DP or traditional personal computing.

But it is very unlikely that the paradigm of new information management will derive from conventional IT vendors or consultants. The new information management will not need to be fettered by these earlier traditions. It is also necessary to consider the creation of a new information professional (NIP), whose skills are needed to support the development of the new paradigm.

Barriers to clarification

It is essential to be able to clarify the distinction between *data* and *information*. This is a distinction that is almost taken for granted among professions such as information science, yet it is one of the neglected themes in practical business information management. But, if this is essential, why has it been so difficult to achieve clarity in the minds of key groups? Why is it routinely:

● completely ignored?
● treated incorrectly or inappropriately especially in day-to-day speech?

There are several possible answers to these questions:

1 It is an area where the underlying concepts are confused, especially across different disciplines and professions. As a result there are genuinely different meanings given to the terms in different contexts.
2 The technology associated with information has a vast vendor, consultant and purchaser drive; there is much less commercial drive behind information itself.

3   Data and information are often intangibles. Many people, including many managers, feel uncomfortable with intangibles.

Some professions depend heavily on data and information, yet if their professional education and training syllabuses are examined very little relating to the body of academic work about these subjects will be found in them.

Attempts at definition

Many problems stem from *no clearly understood and commonly agreed definition of information.* Analysis of only a small part of the writing on information will quickly yield ten, twenty or more definitions of information, largely incompatible with each other.

The most common misunderstanding is to confuse information with data. Data is inert, lifeless, unprocessed. The word information derives from the Latin word meaning 'giving shape to'. Information is data that has been given shape. Most commonly it is described as data plus meaning.

The following useful definitions are taken from BS 3527, Part 1, 1976:

- *Data*: 'A representation of facts, concepts, or instructions in a formalized manner suitable for communication, interpretation, or processing by humans or by automatic means'.
- *Information*: 'The meaning that a human assigns to data by means of conventions used in their presentation'.

Information is data plus the meaning which *has to be a result of human action.* Most information systems are misnamed: they are data systems. Most information technology is misnamed: it is primarily data technology.

The myth of the information age

It is so widely claimed that we are now entering 'the information age', that it has become near-ritualistic for IT industry speakers to start off their presentations with reference to it.

But there are challenges to the idea that we are in the middle of an information revolution. Beniger (1987) points out that a real information revolution took place in the 1830s–1870s, as a result of the increasing problems of running a complex rail network. In particular, this was brought to attention through the rapid growth in serious train crashes. The most obvious effect of this revolution was the standardization of Railway Time.

Since 1949, it is perhaps less appropriate to refer to an information revolution, but rather to an electronic revolution. Electronics has made products:

- smaller;
- faster;
- cheaper;
- more reliable.

But, in contrast to the nineteenth century, there have been surprisingly few inventions of wholly new products in the business IT area. The word processor is a faster, more reliable typewriter. The spreadsheet was modelled on its manual counterpart. As Marshall McLuhan pointed out, inventions are often initially used to reproduce what was already there, and it takes time for the new product to achieve an innovative function.

Data explosion

Far from experiencing an increase in information in recent years, what has actually taken place is a *data explosion*. The outpourings of EPOS machines, of document image processing, of mobile data capture terminals, as well as of PCs and mainframes, all this adds up to a proliferation of data.

But data and information do not necessarily progress together in an upward linear relationship. Arguably, as data expands, there is actually a reduction not just in the relative level of information but even in its absolute level. There is much more irrelevant data – the meaningful information is now harder to find.

Overload and shortage

Many individuals feel that information is a barrier to their personal or team effectiveness. In some cases, the problem is too much – *overload*. In others it is too little – *shortages.*

In fact these terms are used loosely. In relation to the earlier definitions, overload is most typical in relation to data. We have so many different inputs of data now in most societies and organizations, that it actually becomes harder to extract the useful information. So it is increasingly common to find:

DATA OVERLOAD
+
INFORMATION SHORTAGE

Arguably, the central problem today is data overload. This has been particularly clearly analysed by Klapp: 'Information overload challenges the faith of classic liberalism that ever larger amounts of information – however noisy, trivial and banal – processed, packaged and computerized – add up to progress' (Klapp, 1986).

Klapp identified the following causes of information overload:

- loudness;
- disconnectedness;
- bad complexity;
- decoding difficulty;
- clutter of communication;
- lack of feedback;
- stylistic noise;
- pseudo-information;
- sheer overload.

This is not even a new problem. Nyce and Kahn describe the problems faced by Vannevar Bush, who subsequently went on in 1945 as the US Chief Scientist to propose the concept of hypertext: 'From 1932 Bush was occupied with how to find material among the proliferation of print. In 1866 Mendel's concise paper on genetics (which forms the basis of all our understanding of inheritance) had vanished unread into "the literature" not to emerge for decades' (Nyce and Kahn, 1992).

Many of the proponents of the Information Superhighway and of the general use of multimedia appear to be oblivious to the problem of information overload, yet it is becoming a managerial and perhaps even a social problem. One senior figure in the UK IT industry recently gave a presentation which correctly identified the problem of long working hours by many managers. In a later part of the presentation he described his own personal seven-day-a-week use of e-mail, even from home on Sundays. Yet arguably such usage constitutes a form of overload with ramifications running far beyond the office.

There are, however, some signs that the problem is recognized. For example, Peters and Austin (1985) describe simplification methods at Marks and Spencer in terms which suggest the company is preoccupied with avoiding information overload:

1 Sensible approximation – the price of perfection is prohibitive.
2 Reporting by exception (only when absolutely necessary).
3 Manuals – no attempt is made to legislate for every contingency and every eventuality.
4 Decategorization – people have been removed from watertight compartments and placed in general categories.
5 People can be trusted, so checks can be eliminated.

What is reality? When we move from analogue to digital?

Another major problem in the concept of the information age relates to the nature of reality. If we suppose there is some sort of objective reality, then much of what we know about that reality is entirely second-hand. We have never directly experienced the oceans of Antarctica or the New York Stock Exchange, but we have seen them on television.

In an accounting environment, a finance director is very unlikely to have physically seen the purchase of an office desk, or the invoice relating to it. The director might, if pressed, be able to find a member of staff who could look up the transaction on a tabulation or via a VDU. But this emphasizes just how far removed he or she is from the 'real' transaction.

The question of 'what is reality?' cannot therefore be addressed purely by reference to scientific concepts. Reality involves:

● philosophy – the nature of knowledge;
● psychology – the impact of the individual;
● sociology – the individual within a group or culture.

Let us for the moment assume that there is a concept of reality, even though this is disputed strongly by some scientists, some philosophers and some   *45* linguists. In so far as we use the concept of objective reality, we know that we interact with this reality via our senses of vision, hearing, touch, taste and smell. Traditional scientific thinking characterizes the communication of data *from* an external object *to* our senses via *analogue* methods such as sound waves or light waves. The object is not analogue, but the channels of natural communication are.

We have now developed digital techniques which can mimic or reproduce analogue communications:

- Digitalization involves fragmentation – breaking up something that was whole, then re-creating it as a facsimile of the original.
- Digitalization enables many different media to be integrated.
- Digitalization is a great help in editing and amending.
- Digitalization enables efficient communication of data.

But, even in a tiny way, digitalization loses some of the essence of the original. At worst it makes it easy to alter or forge the original. Perhaps of greatest concern is the potential for confusion between the digital image as representation, and the actual reality. Consider the following:

> A railway system operates computer tracking of trains and calculates the estimated arrival times at destinations. Information Centres in railway stations have continuous access to these arrival times. There are also large display panels for the public.
> A public display panel shows the 19:25 train due to arrive at 10:25. Someone awaiting the train at 19:19 will probably judge that this is a technical error, so the real arrival time is expected to be 19:25.
> At 19:27 there is no sign of the train, so it is appropriate to go to the Information Centre. The clerk in the information centre checks on the screen and say that 'The train arrived at 19:24 at Platform 5'. The great irony is that Platform 5 is actually visible from the Information Centre. There is clearly no train there.
> The train actually arrived at 19:39.

The railway system has two parallel and inaccurate digital information systems. 'Reality' can be determined by walking to look at the platform. The clerk relied on a digital system even where a quick glance could have confirmed the digital system was an inadequate representation of reality.

Objective reality?

There is currently an enormous argument in the philosophy of science between objectivists, who believe there is a real external world, and science is about 'discovering' what that real world is, and social constructivists, who believe that at any given time in history, science and its findings cannot be divorced from the social climate and culture within which it works and that science is therefore primarily a social construct.

This is not the place to further this debate, but the strength of feeling between the two sides illustrates the depths of emotion that exist in relation to objectivity and subjectivity in science. It is a tragedy that we are not having this same emotionally charged discussion about data, information, knowledge and wisdom in a business context because the longer we fail to do so, the longer we expend time, energy and investment in ways which due to our clouded thinking will not yield us, our businesses, or our societies real benefit.

Hard and soft data

In any organization, there are a number of clearly identifiable aspects of management:

- ensuring the operational tasks run smoothly;
- analysing future trends, opportunities, markets, customer needs etc. in the light of current operational capability;
- taking decisions on long- and short-term strategies and tactics;
- taking action to implement these decisions i.e. to amend the scope or nature of the current operational tasks.

At all of these stages, considerable use is made of a variety of data. This can be defined on a spectrum from hard to soft. Hard data tends to be precise and measurable, representing some real-world events that can be represented reasonably accurately by the measurement. For example, measurements of temperature in the air (10°C), or height of a person (1.8m), would be regarded by most people as fairly objective descriptions.

On the other hand, soft data may:

1 Represent events or objects, which by their very nature are difficult to measure or even to describe precisely, for example the subject of 'kindness'.
2 Be imprecise measures or description of objects and events that could in principle be objectively described. We can ask whether a person we have not met yet is 'tall' or 'short'; this would be a much softer type of description than the answer, 'she is 1.8 metres'.

In the world of business, throughout the whole of history there has been an understandable focus on the tangible, and on the measurable. Profit and loss can be measured, based on the particular accounting convention prevailing in a given culture or society. Levels of goods in stock can be measured, although it may be much more difficult, at least in some businesses, to estimate either the physical condition of the stock, or its current real value.

It is noteworthy that the very invention of writing around 3200BC in the Middle East was to support accountancy, rather than literary, legal, artistic or religious purposes:

> Writing was invented in order to record business activities in the early Near East. With the growth of centralized economies the officials of palaces and temples needed to be able to keep track of the amounts of grain and numbers of sheep and cattle which were entering or leaving their stores and farms. It was impossible to rely on a man's memory for every detail, and a new method was needed to keep reliable records (Walker, 1987).

Ever since Babylonian times, good management has always involved acquiring and considering data along the full range between hard and soft. In reality, the distinction is much less clear-cut than the terms suggest. For example, to someone brought up with Anglo-Saxon measurements, neither '10 degrees Celsius' nor '1.8 metres high' actually carries much meaning at all. And in reality neither of these is as exact as it seems. Does 1.8 metres mean 1.80000 metres, or is it anywhere between 1.750 and 1.849 metres? The temperature may average 10 degrees or have a peak of 10 degrees, but for most of the time it will be moving up and down. The significance of this is to point out that even hard data needs to be fit for a purpose and that this varies with the information purpose which it serves.

The need for fundamental breakthrough in information management

At the moment we are in the information equivalent of the pre-Galileo, pre-Newton, pre-Descartes, pre-Faraday state of physical sciences. We simply have not had the fundamental breakthrough needed in information management.

Where will this fundamental breakthrough come from? There must be some doubt as to whether it will come from a western culture, or (more specifically) an Anglo-Saxon culture. The very drivers that have fuelled the success of the west in the scientific area and during the first two industrial revolutions (of manufacturing and then of scientific management), may actually hamper the west in the information revolution.

The industrial revolutions were based on a fragmented, competitive, engineering-led approach. There is a distinct possibility that the information revolution will be led by holistic, co-operative, culturally led approaches. It is in these areas that some eastern societies, particularly those that are based on Chinese culture and scripts, may well have distinct competitive advantage. Is it a coincidence that one of the more profound works on information management is the last 50 years is by an Indian? (Ranganathan, 1957); Ranganathan produced a so-called colon classification, for classifying library materials, based around five 'fundamental facets': personality, matter, energy, space, time.

Informacy

We lack the intellectual frameworks to deal with the problems of data overload. Such frameworks need to be created, and the equivalent of Shoshana Zuboff's informating is clearly 'informacy'. But we need to be very aware of the constraints in this enterprise. One of the most profound critics of the conventional wisdom is Theodore Roszak (1988) – a professor of history.

The core managerial competency needed is currently not even under systematic development. We call this 'Informacy', to set alongside literacy and numeracy. This is the art and science of the management and organization of information and knowledge.

In a recent review, Taylor and Farrell (1994) propose four areas in which information managers need skills:

- information engineering;
- information organization management;
- information psychology;
- the sociology of information.

It would certainly be possible to add to this information politics (McGee and Prusak, 1993) and information economics (Johnson, 1993), to provide an idea of the range of disciplines that are needed to support informacy.

Potential frameworks – a perspective on fads

In the context of this generally gloomy perspective, it may be reasonable to ask whether there are any approaches or frameworks that might be capable of providing either short-term relief or acting as a basis for the longer-term breakthrough.

One of the features of management thinking generally over the last 100 years has been a preoccupation with 'silver bullet' solutions – the search for a quick-acting managerial panacea. Such preoccupations were just as common in 1894 as they are in 1994. This mostly reflects the intrinsic difficulty of managing organizations. The task is difficult because it is immersed in uncertainty and risk, lacking generally applicable theories and practices, and dominated by interlocking problems of structure, organization, strategy, people and resources.

In earlier centuries, managing this uncertainty at both personal and state levels led to widespread interest in extra-rational methods of forecasting and advice. In the Roman period, a key managerial diagnostic tool was the examination of chicken livers. In the early Middle Ages in Britain, great store was set on the prophecies of Merlin. Much of this extra-rational behaviour has continued into the twentieth century with the pursuit of managerial 'fads'. These are hyped up panaceas to complex management problems that gain audiences in the retelling. A typical example was Peters and Waterman's *In Search of Excellence*. This was at the time of publication a well-argued and in many ways soundly researched book. Though it contained little that had not already been identified in management research, it argued persuasively and packaged the arguments attractively.

It was always implausible that any set of generalized management panaceas would apply from Alabama to Accrington let alone across airlines and air-conditioning. But not only did the book spawn a movement with a high priest (Tom Peters himself), the movement continued in being long after the weaknesses in the original text had been exposed, and when the quality of research that had supported the original text did not seem to be repeated in subsequent work.

The 'excellence fad' is now being followed by the 'reengineering fad'. And these are just two in a lengthy tradition of such fads. This is not to say that the fads are worthless. Both 'excellence' and 're-engineering' have valuable core

49

messages for the long term. The problem is that when the fad-led movement dies, the valuable core messages may become lost or discredited.

Searching for a foundation – engineering?

The metaphor adopted by computing's main UK professional body, the British Computer Society (BCS), is that of engineering. The software developer is a software engineer. The BCS member can become eligible to become a chartered engineer. Now this is not to criticize either the engineering profession in general, or the software engineer in particular. Both are important, in their place. But the mistake is to ignore other professions that could act as metaphors.

The whole history of computing in the UK has inexorably derived from the scientific and engineering tradition. One of the reasons for this is the leading role that the UK played in the technological developments of computers, particularly in the 1950s. The engineering approach to information systems is not 'wrong' – its weaknesses only become apparent if more is expected of it than it is capable of delivering.

Searching for a foundation – the systems approach?

One of the most promising domains to support informacy is the general systems approach. But it is essential to point out that this approach was a core management fad of the 1960s. It actually had many opponents at that time, and when during the early 1970s the practical attempts to implement it fell into disfavour, relatively few mourned either its business or intellectual decease.

However, we need to be clear why the general systems approach failed in a business context:

1 It was actually talked about a great deal more than it was implemented. It was less a failure of implementation than a failure to be implemented very much at all.
2 Its failures (or perceived failures) were often high profile, e.g. attempts to use it in inner city planning, or in the US leadership of the Vietnam War, or to support Allende's government in Chile.
3 It was an approach that called for a radical and holistic perspective. Though these were fashionable words in the society of 1968 in much of the western world, they did not appeal at that time to many of the older managers at the top levels of organizations.
4 The economic climate of the 1960s was one of growth, of overheating rather than recession, of labour shortages and full employment. This was consistent with a fairly conservative style of management and organization. Executives and managers could be successful without radical and holistic approaches. There was therefore no compelling business driver for radical, systems-led change.

Although the systems approach appears to have been long since managerially discredited, some of its advocates have been unwavering in their support for the approach for the last 30 years.

There have also been explicit attempts to re-package the systems approach, most notably by Peter Senge (1990) of the Massachusetts Institute of Technology in his book *The Fifth Discipline*. Although Senge, rather unfortunately, attempts to hypothecate the generic term 'systems thinking' to describe his own particular systems methodology, his work is largely a restating of the systems approach, drawing on system dynamics and more indirectly from the socio-technical theories of the 1960s.

Searching for a foundation – management cybernetics?

During the 1960s in particular, much promise was offered by the then emerging discipline of cybernetics. In the UK the most profound exponent of the cybernetic approach to management was Stafford Beer (1981) who outlined (in *Brain of the Firm*) an idealized model of how an enterprise could reorganize itself along cybernetic lines, a theme which he developed in his subsequent works.

Beer's writings are as profound now as when they were first written, but in the intervening period there unfortunately has been relatively little direct attempt to implement them in actual business situations. The promise therefore remains largely unfulfilled in practice. The single large-scale attempt to implement Beer's ideas was in the Chile of President Allende. Supported by Allende, and with Finance Minister Fernando Flores as day-to-day champion, significant steps forward were made in seeing Beer's vision implemented to run a government. The assassination of Allende and overthrow of his government brought the innovation to an abrupt halt.

As the 'hard' systems approach, based on mechanistic application of the engineering methodology, came under increasing attack, a new methodology emerged from the work of Peter Checkland (1981) at Lancaster University. His 'soft systems approach' attracted a greater critical mass of adherents in the academic world than Beer's cybernetic approach had been able to do, and this in turn meant a wider recognition in the business community of the benefits of the soft systems approach. However, while the soft systems approach overcomes some of the weaknesses of the hard systems approach, it also remains an incomplete solution.

Searching for a foundation – philosophy and linguistics?

Reviewing the academic disciplines that may underpin the information revolution, a central role could well be played by philosophy. For several thousands of years philosophy has addressed fundamental issues of being, of knowledge, of meaning and of truth. 'Our knowledge resides in the signs we use and how we use them. It would be surprising, therefore, if the study of information did not raise serious philosophical problems' (Stamper, 1973).

Another and much newer discipline that could contribute is the whole area of media studies. This discipline, which has evolved in part out of sociology, is preoccupied with the efficiency and effectiveness of communications in both a technical and psychological sense. It tends to take a broad-based, multi-disciplinary perspective on communications. It is not a discipline that has been over-focused on the business context, but its contribution has yet perhaps to be made here.

The next source of inspiration for a methodology to underpin information systems development came from an apparently surprising quarter. Ever since the philosopher Wittgenstein had examined language before the Second World War, there had been a school of linguistic philosophy emerging that culminated in Searle's work on the action language perspective.

Then in similar vein, the 1970s saw an upsurge of interest in radical approaches to literary criticism. These approaches were popularized by, among others, Jaques Derrida in France and Umberto Eco in Italy, but both authors' works became readily available in the Anglo-Saxon world as well, and were highly influential – as well as very controversial.

This approach was dubbed 'post-structuralist', as it challenged the earlier work of structuralists such as Lévi-Strauss. It was particularly critical of the concept of 'objective' reality.

The formal study of language draws on at least two disciplines: linguistics (the study of human speech); and semiotics (the science of signs).

The fashionable interest in post-structuralism led to a resurgence of interest in semiotics in particular, and it was perhaps inevitable that this would eventually find its way into the information systems field. This was primarily led from the French and Italian heartlands of post-structuralism. One of the first English books drawing on this perspective was by Liebenau and Backhouse, who argued strongly that semiotics should be *the* underpinning discipline for information systems: 'We can resist the allure of technology by recognizing that business is carried out using language and that semiotics offers the means to specify what the organization does in a better way' (Liebenau and Backhouse, 1990).

Winograd and Flores (1986) reviewed and drew on post-structuralism, though their central focus was on the action-language perspective embedded in innovative products such as 'the coordinator', one of the first commercial groupware products.

Information resource management

One perspective that takes an information-based stance is that of information resource management (IRM). This derives essentially from the world of information science and librarianship, with strong elements from general business management. IRM focuses on information needs, storage, retrieval, indexing and user-interface. Information technology is a means, not a driving force.

Information resource management, however, has not made a major impact on business thinking or practice. Eaton and Bawden (1991) identify some of the reasons why information cannot be treated wholly like the more conventional management resources.

A new discipline?

It is unlikely that any one of the various existing approaches to information systems are likely to be able to produce a single 'right' way, either now or in the future.

This is not to say that a new discipline or body of knowledge might not evolve or emerge, however, which could provide us with a more relevant and more comprehensive framework than those currently available. This discipline (information management) may continue to be eclectic and lacking a coherent core body of thinking; perhaps it must by its nature be a true cross-disciplinary domain with relatively little of its own unique core thinking. However, if there is to be a new discipline covering this field, furthering the academic work already undertaken by departments such as my own, what would its characteristics be?

As an academic subject, information management is on the fringes of economics, of psychology, of sociology, of science policy, of business studies and even (most curiously) of informatics.

The closest profession and academic discipline to embrace information management is information science. But the work of information science has not received the recognition by business that it deserves. The profession of information science collectively and individually perhaps does not have sufficient will or motivation to advocate its own cause successfully against the much stronger commercially driven pressures of the IT professions.

Roots in existing information-oriented professions

There are at least three other routes to promoting the subject of information management, and particularly competencies in it. One is creating 'hybrid managers', who span IM and other disciplines.

Another is addressing the needs of cognate professions, for example accounting and marketing. For example, this could involve its formal study within the professional syllabuses of those disciplines.

A third is to persuade and support strategic management in recognizing the significance of IM, for example via awareness and educational programmes.

All three of these are of importance, but even if all three approaches are taken together this is unlikely to be able to produce the critical mass of support and awareness needed for change.

New information professional

Unless some remarkable transformation takes place quickly, it is very unlikely that the current IT professional will transmute into the new information professional (NIP). Partly this is due to inappropriate personal characteristics. A strongly rational analytical, convergent personality – common in IT – is not very appropriate for the NIP. Secondly, the IT profession has a baggage of customs and practices that could be antagonistic to the NIP. The British Computer Society has achieved chartered engineer status for some of its members. The NIP needs to be much more like an architect than an engineer.

Many IT people ask 'how can we improve the link between the IT professional and the business?' An answer to this is to recognize that it is information and its use which is the vital contribution made by IT to the business, hence *53* the need to promote a new category of intermediary – the new information professional.

There is rarely any competitive advantage arising purely from the deployment of IT itself. Competitive advantage primarily derives through the ways that IT transforms the delivery of information and hence the speed, effectiveness and efficiency of the business. So asking about the IT/business gap is, quite simply, focusing on the old agenda. The new agenda is about the technology – information – business link. The NIP has therefore to be skilled in the disciplines which bridge this gap: those of synthesis, persuasion, commercial judgement and the knowledge of how information can make a difference. The new professionals will need to be able to understand the goals of the manager in a way which will enable them to exploit and interpret the facilities of the technology to support and enhance the manager's judgement, not only in speed and quantity but also in quality.

Conditions for change

What events are likely to create the conditions under which the new theory of information will emerge? The most likely candidate is a crisis. Currently the assumption persists that all the problems of computer systems development are soluble within the present systems development paradigm. It is simply a matter of better tools, 'better technology', better (more IT aware) business managers, getting more business literate IT staff and better evaluation of benefits. Sooner or later when all these partial and incremental solutions have been exhausted, one or more major breakdowns in information systems may fan the flames of crisis. Out of this crisis will develop intensive and long overdue research into information management. As happened with a number of important innovations in the Second World War, the pressure of the war itself forced change and innovation.

In many ways, this strategic diagnosis is extremely pessimistic, and is deliberately so. It is impossible to underestimate the damage being done by the confusion of data and information. The problems of information overload are approaching epidemic proportions. The inability of western societies to resolve the informational dimensions of the technology that will support a future information revolution, could be of profound strategic significance to whole societies if we remain incapable of recognizing the distinctions between data and information and between analysis and judgement.

The optimists in this area will typically point to innovations including:

- use of artificial intelligence;
- improved methods of data storage and retrieval;
- better techniques for handling 'soft' data;
- use of software agents that can learn to mimic a user's desired search, filtering and retrieval behaviours.

The aim here is not to decry such technical innovations. But it cannot be known if any of these tools of data handling will in fact alleviate the information crisis. It can also be argued that much of the problem lies in inadequate skills and competence in managing information. Many organizations are working hard on increasing such skills and awareness but this often relates much more to the 'hard' information area than the 'soft'.

CONCLUSION

The first 40 years of business computing has, quite naturally, been preoccupied with the introduction and development of new systems. Even where information systems have been stable from a business need and a software perspective, they have needed upgrading and replacement due to advances in hardware, particularly improvements in its performance and reduction in its cost.

As the move towards client-server architecture takes place, with the introduction of scalable hardware architectures for both PCs and Unix machines, the need for continuous upgrading and replacement of information systems will reduce. The maintenance function will begin to dominate the world of IT professionals, probably involving re-usable objects. The prestige associated with the introduction of wholly new systems and of major upgrades is likely to be reduced.

The continuation of crises in what is perceived as information businesses will eventually precipitate another real information revolution along the lines that happened in 1830–70 as a result of control crises and rail crashes. This will need a new information profession.

This is the environment in which a gradual shift of roles from the IT professional (concerned with *building* systems) to the new information professional (concerned with *exploiting* the information in systems) will take place.

REFERENCES

Beer, S. (1981), *Brain of the Firm*, 2nd edn, Chichester: John Wiley.

Beniger, J.R. (1987), *The Control Revolution*, Cambridge, MA: Harvard University Press.

Checkland, P. (1981), *Systems Thinking, Systems Practice*, Chichester: John Wiley.

Eaton, J.J. and Bawden, D. (1991), 'What Kind of Resource is Information?' *International Journal of Information Management*, **11**, pp. 156–65.

Espejo, R. and Harnden, R. (1989), *The Viable System Model – Interpretations and Applications of Stafford Beer's VSM*, Chichester: John Wiley.

Johnson, N. (ed.) (1993), *The Knowledge Economy*, Nashville, TN: Institute for Information Studies.

Klapp, O.E. (1986), *Overload and Boredom*, New York: Greenwood Press.

Leach, G. (1974), *Semantics*, Harmondsworth: Penguin.

Liebenau, J. and Backhouse, J. (1990), *Understanding Information – An Introduction,* London: Macmillan.

McGee, J.V. and Prusak, L. (1993), *Managing Information Strategically*, New York: John Wiley.

Nyce, J.M. and Kahn, P. (eds) (1992), *From Memex to Hypertext: Vannevar Bush and the Mind's Machine*, New York: Academic Press.

Peters, T. and Austin, N. (1985), *A Passion for Excellence*, London: Collins.

Ranganathan, S.R. (1957), *Prolegomena to Library Classification*, London: Library Association.

Roszak, T. (1988), *The Cult of Information – The Folklore of Computers and the True Art of Thinking*, London: Paladin.

Senge, P. (1990), *The Fifth Discipline*, New York: Doubleday.

Stamper, R. (1973), *Information in Business and Administrative Systems*, London: B.T. Batsford.

Taylor, A. and Farrell, S. (1994), *Information Management for Business*, London: Aslib.

Walker, C.B.F. (1987), *Cuneiform*, London: British Museum Publications.

Winograd, T. and Flores, F. (1986), *Understanding Computers and Cognition: A New Foundation for Design*, Reading, MA: Addison-Wesley.

Part II

THE TECHNOLOGY ANGLE

This part of the book covers two areas where technology can support the ideas discussed in Part I. In the first chapter, Julia Parsons discusses the process view of business from the standpoint of the tools and techniques available to support the necessary analysis and shows where information management fits into this puzzle.

In the second chapter, Bill Thom of Interleaf, who has been involved with text technologies for many years, describes some examples of how information can be managed using the emerging hypertext-based technologies.

4 Information – the fourth resource

Julia Parsons

OVERVIEW

Just as the concept of information management (IM) has developed over the last decade, so the tools and techniques to assist in implementing good IM have also grown both in number and variety. In the 1960s and early 1970s, information technology (IT) or data processing as it was known at the time, was starting to find its way into organizations. Initially, this tended to be applied in an *ad hoc* manner, with each programmer reinventing the wheel every time a system was built. As it was recognized that there was some commonality in this exercise, so the methods were formalized and methodologies were born.

Information management is a term which is only now starting to gain a place in common usage. IM is still confused with IT, probably as a result of the similarity of the terms. However, IM is much broader and includes all aspects of handling information. This includes the procedural and clerical aspects as well as any kind of technology that might be involved, not forgetting the most important aspect – the human element.

IM includes the management of information in any form, particularly the written form. Documents, whether on paper, electronic or image form a major part of the information that today's technologies address. Michael H. Kay of ICL refers to five different types of information – operational, management, professional, work group and historical, where each type should be treated differently because their contribution to competitive advantage is different. This is important in focusing IM expenditure on information which has a direct effect on the competitiveness of the business itself. Most IT strategies have concentrated on operational information, with some attention paid to management information, whereas the expenditure on technological support for professional knowledge, work group communication or historical information is low even when major savings can be achieved.

Several methodologies in IM and the implementation of supporting technologies are discussed in the next section. In summary, most approaches include some of the steps mentioned below:

- review current process in terms of what it is trying to achieve;
- model it to aid communication;
- 'formulate' improvements;
- redesign the process;
- investigate possible technology support;
- consider the change management aspects;
- implement new process and supporting technology;
- monitor, continue to re-evaluate and continue to redesign.

This chapter gives an overview of some of the myriad tools, methodologies and techniques which may be used to assist in the successful implementation of IM, whether as part of a business process re-engineering (BPR) activity or not. It is intended to provide a route map for those seeking information on what is available, as opposed to a definitive description of particular products. It is hoped that the reader will have been stimulated into action by the other chapters in this book and that this chapter will supply the starting point for those embarking on the exciting and rewarding road towards managing their information effectively.

Information has been referred to as 'the fourth resource' after money, people and property/equipment – all of which have their management disciplines in financial management, human resources and facilities management. As has been described elsewhere, it is vital to manage the increasingly important resource of information. I believe that as some of the concepts of IM become widespread, we will see the nature of work change dramatically, as is already apparent from some examples of IM associated with BPR, such as teleworking and the virtual organization.

The technology has enabled completely different ways of working, by facilitating the transfer of and access to information. With globalization, economic pressure, corporate change and the recession, decentralization and rationalization have occurred to export jobs or permanently destroy them. Small groups of the self-employed have established themselves in outlying relatively inaccessible areas of the country from the Highlands of Scotland to Cornwall as 'telecottage' groups, using telecommunications to provide services to a wide range of clients. The South East's financial sector has already experienced the effect of this.

Offshore telecentres are also a growth area in providing cheap electronically based services. For example, high calibre bulk data entry can enable source documents to be transmitted to the Philippines where, given the time difference, the work can be keyed and returned during the client's off-hours night shift.

A virtual organization is a network of independent groups linked by the free flow of information. There is no hierarchy, no central office and no vertical integration, just the skills and resources needed to do a specific job. By setting up a new virtual organization to address each business opportunity, the mix of skills is always ideal. As projects develop, so does the virtual organization, gaining and losing partners as appropriate. When the project is complete the organization is disbanded, or may live on in the information repository of its principals.

Information is the key element in virtual organizations because it is the intellect, knowledge and skills of its members which are the organization's most valuable asset. This means that information and its use will become paramount and hence information will be recognized as the first *resource*. Consequently, its management should not be left to chance and solutions developed in an *ad hoc* way.

In support of IM there are many tools and methodologies available, with more regularly arriving on the market. They have specific purposes such as traditional IT systems design, process modelling or helping to generate the operational system itself, although this delineation is starting to blur as suppliers attempt to provide the all-encompassing product. Choosing the right tool or methodology to solve your business problem starts with an understanding of what is available, then refining your requirements in order to identify the most appropriate solution. It is essential to choose the right tool for the job.

Information management and its relationship to BPR

The advent of business process reengineering has had a significant impact on information managers because it has required them to think rigorously and logically about the soft information associated with key business processes in a way which is new in many cases. Among senior managers it has inspired an interest in information as part of the exercise of dramatically rethinking the way in which an organization works (see also B. Cronin's chapter in this book). As with the organization and methods (O&M) techniques of work measurement, flowcharting and work study, no technique, tool or methodology alone can make a success of your IM strategy. The intelligent application of these tools is the key to achieving the benefits promised by good IM.

But is IM an art or a science? The word 'methodology' is described in the *Concise Oxford Dictionary* as 'the science of method'. Strictly speaking, a methodology is more than a method, it is the study or interest in method. In the systems development environment, a methodology is commonly held to be a set of rules about how one goes about developing systems. The methodology becomes a *modus operandi* which can be applied to form a standard approach. The implication is that, if it is applied consistently, then the results will be predictable, as with a scientific experiment.

Unfortunately the real world of the office environment is frequently more of a disorganization than an organization. While there may be rules and procedures laid down, it is common to find that staff have developed short cuts and work-arounds in practice. Therefore a methodology alone cannot guarantee success. In other words, the skilled analyst will always be part of the equation. Hence, I believe that IM is both an art and a science and the combination of the right tools and techniques in the hands of a skilled practitioner   *61* leads directly to success.

The remaining sections of this chapter cover the management of information in relation to analysing, modelling, and changing organizational processes, and some of the methodologies available to save reinventing the wheel and an overview of process modelling tools which can assist in streamlining the way your organization works. Process modelling tools provide a graphical means of describing the current information flows, as an aid to identifying what can be changed to make improvements.

The diagram in Figure 4.1 indicates the scope of process modelling tools and methodologies in relation to the entire process of IM.

The dotted box indicates the potential scope of the information manager: clearly the tools and techiques available range from almost the level of business strategy at the high level to system development methods at the lower end, taking in techniques such as information mapping and others *en route*. The main thrust of this article is the tools and techniques relevant to the middle ground.

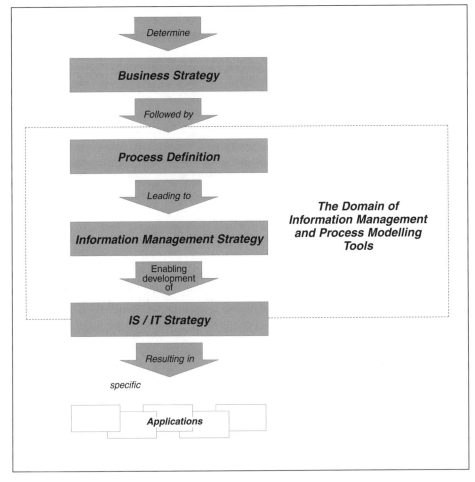

Figure 4.1   The domain of IM and process modelling tools

MANAGEMENT OF INFORMATION

How does an organization start to manage its information better, and how can it gain the dramatic benefits to be achieved from streamlining its processes? There are two schools of thought in terms of approaching the management of information within an organization.

The bottom-up approach

The first school of thought is the traditional method of the 'bottom-up' approach. This is where the current 'system' of policies, standards, processes, procedures and computer systems is analysed in detail to provide the basis for change. The type of change usually achieved with this method is incremental, with no dramatic re-engineering of the processes involved but the application of automation to certain parts of the process, perhaps automating current manual procedures.

This might be perfectly valid, if the process itself is sound and running effectively. Dramatic change should never be instigated for its own sake. While the benefits may be smaller than in a complete overhaul of the business, the risks are generally lower since the changes are easier to implement. However, there is a particular risk with this approach in that concentrating on the current processes may result in little or no improvement if the underlying processes themselves are at fault. The bottom-up approach is commonly applied to routine office processes, where process modelling tools are used to map the current procedures and then as the basis for designing new, improved processes and document flow. The risk is that opportunities are overlooked and the resulting process may be only a quicker version of the current procedure. As Michael Hammer, credited as the initiator of BPR, is often quoted as saying, 'Don't automate, obliterate'.

This problem of automating the wrong thing occurred in the early days of IT, where manual systems were religiously automated only to find the automation itself actually changed the nature of the requirement, resulting in inefficient systems which did not deliver the full benefits promised by automation. Experience taught users and developers that the implementation of computer systems would change the tasks that staff performed, causing information to be treated in completely new ways. A simple example of this was the use of on-line enquiries to provide information for decision-making, rather than voluminous hard-copy reports.

A variation of the bottom-up approach is to model the current 'system' and use this as means to redesign the processes, resulting in a new model of how the 'system' could work. The new design can vary from the current system according to the objectives of the exercise and the risk aversion level of the organization.

From the IM perspective also the bottom-up approach has certain disadvantages. Information is often kept in islands of information, which may have few or no links between them. As our 1994 information management survey (Touche Ross, 1994) showed, information is often duplicated in different units of the same department and is often re-created rather than being effectively retrieved.   *63*

In all of these cases a bottom-up approach to IM and process improvement may not solve the problems.

The top-down approach

The second approach, associated with BPR, is the 'top-down' method, starting with the equivalent of a blank sheet of paper and deciding the way the organization should work, given its mission in life. This literally starts at the top of an organization in establishing the change imperative, by obtaining executive sponsorship and ensuring visible and committed leadership for the project. It requires the vision to imagine a new way of working and the determination to overcome the obstacles in achieving it.

The top-down approach tends to be applied to the line-of-business or mission critical processes as opposed to the routine office tasks which benefit from the bottom-up approach. Making changes of this type requires a change of attitude throughout the organization, so that it can become a forward-looking, learning organization. Improvements to areas that are core to the business are more likely to result in achieving substantial benefits compared with improving back-office administrative functions, unless the latter result in improved customer service.

Again, looked at from the IM perspective there are considerable benefits to this approach: once the objectives or end results of a process have been agreed it is then less difficult to identify what information is needed to enable these processes to be undertaken and to determine what format, media, and storage/retreival and processing methods are necessary and justifiable.

METHODOLOGIES/TECHNIQUES

Most methodologies consist of checklists, procedures and helpful hints to save reinventing the wheel. This supports the definition that 'a methodology is the body of methods and rules employed by a *science* or discipline'. They are helpful because they give structure to a complex task, produce results in a form which should be intelligible to others and can be repeated.

When I first started my career, there were no such things as methodologies, but, despite this, records repositories, systems and procedures were developed successfully and ran for many years before being replaced. At that time, building systems, using that term in its wider sense, was a mystery to anyone outside the O&M, registry or DP departments. Men in white coats came and asked you what you did and then went away to their ivory tower for some years before emerging triumphant with a result which usually no longer addressed the needs of the business. The direct involvement of users was practically unheard of and sometimes actively discouraged; relevant departments alone had the expertise. Experience of this mysterious activity was learnt on the job and such people commanded high salaries.

It then became apparent that this development knowledge could be communicated more effectively by writing it down. The condensed experience of many man years of 'getting it wrong' has gone into the methodologies which now give guidance on how to get it right.

Techniques that developed in the 1970s and 1980s concentrated on data and data entities. This included such concepts as data modelling, data flow, entity life history modelling, data dictionaries and data structures. Methods such SSADM (Structural Systems Analysis and Design Method), Yourdon and IEF (Information Engineering Facility) combined these techniques into data-oriented methodologies.

As methodologies went, these were rigorous and had to be applied stringently for the technique to work. This also meant that inexperienced staff could follow the technique meticulously and arrive at the correct design for a system. The only problem is that these methodologies were very laborious and great effort was required to arrive at an answer that was obvious to the experienced designer.

Other early methodologies, also usually applied rigorously were those already mentioned such as O&M techniques and others mentioned by Orna in this book. In the field of records management and library science, methods had been unchanged for some decades, while computer-based text management systems usually relied upon computer methodologies. Where OBM methods were applied, the very action of studying someone working, especially with a stop-watch, inevitably caused the process being studied to change, especially if piecework was involved, the so-called 'Hawthorne effect'.

Computer Aided Software Engineering (CASE) tools have been around for the last decade or so and their use to describe an application environment is well established. These tools, such as Excelerator, provide a graphic means of specifying the data elements of the system in terms of stores and how they are changed by processes. The data flow around the proposed system can be shown at different levels and the records and fields of data associated with it can be defined. Again, however, these systems are at the level of data, not of process and information.

These types of tools assist the designer in that they show a graphical representation of the system and help ensure consistency of data so that design errors can be easily spotted. A CASE tool will not design the solution, but will facilitate the process by supporting the designer. A major benefit from using CASE tools for computer systems is that the actual code for the system can be generated directly from the design, as opposed to the traditional method of a designer specifying programs which are then coded by programmers. An example of this is CASE generator from Oracle. The code thus generated still requires to be modified and perfected by the programmer, but the CASE tool removes a significant amount of the repetitive coding of information already specified by the designer.

Business analysis techniques

The business analysis technique (BAT), based on the soft systems methodology, was originated by Professor Peter Checkland at the University of Lancaster and further developed by commercial consultants. It provides a method of understanding and solving business problems and compares the way a business ought to work in the ideal sense with what happens in real life (see also Checkland, 1984). There are four main stages:

- *Stage 1 – produce a business system model.* This consists of defining the set of components that must combine to achieve the business objectives in the form of a logical model. It covers the purpose and performance measures of the system, the system owner, the system beneficiary, who will carry out the main tasks, the processes which transform inputs into outputs and the overall environment in which the system will operate. It describes what the system is. An activity model is then produced that describes the activities which must logically take place to satisfy the business system definition. Activity models are built by writing down the set of activities in bubbles and showing the logical dependencies between them as arrows. They describe what the system does.
- *Stage 2 – characteristics of the business system.* This consists of identifying more details about the business system in terms of important characteristics such as information, communications and organizational structure.
- *Stage 3 – comparing the model to the real world.* This is an assessment of how closely the current activities match up to the ideal and how well information needs are being met. The results of this stage are conclusions and recommendations on what needs to be changed, so that the business can more closely resemble the ideal.
- *Stage 4 – Implement.* The fourth stage consists of implementing the required changes to bring about the new system.

This methodology is particularly helpful from the point of view of IM because the process of defining the system in stage 1 explicitly includes the definition of the information (and, subsequently, data) necessary and sufficient to carry out the processes of the system.

Process modelling related methodologies

Almost every product supplier and every consultancy involved in implementing systems will have their own methodology. I include a selection to indicate the sorts of things that comprise a methodology.

Praxis's STRIM process modelling method

Praxis is the software engineering division of Touche Ross. STRIM originated as part of the work done on the UK Alvey Programme in 1986 for ICL. The method has two phases. The first uses two diagrammatic languages to capture the results of information gathering, role activity diagrams (RADs, described further in the 'Processing Modelling section') which focus on the process, and entity relationship attributes (ERA) models which focus on the data. The second stage uses a textual language (the STRIM process modelling language – SPML) to describe the processes in a standard form which will facilitate consistency checking and enactment of the process. This textual structured language contains all the information necessary to derive traditional data-flow diagrams, entity life histories and entity relationship models.

STRIM is based on five basic elements:

1 *Business goals*. The model must show how the process is achieving the goals.
2 *Constraints*. This is the identification of the business rules as reflected by the policies and procedures within an organization, as well as the standards it maintains and the responsibilities and delegation levels.
3 *Roles*. The parts that people play in the process.
4 *Activities*. This consists of what individuals do to achieve the goals the organization sets itself and how these are split over various roles.
5 *Interactions*. This is how individuals within groups work collaboratively in order to get the job done.

Interesting by its absence from the above list is data. In Praxis's experience, the *true information* necessary to a process is readily revealed by examining the process alone. Much of the data in an organization is the record of the status of a process or is a way of implementing an interaction. However, traditional entity modelling has a part to play in the STRIM methodology as a complementary method for establishing the entities that need to be captured in the record of the process.

IBM

IBM has developed a proprietory methodology which begins by understanding the real business problem. This involves knowing what the problem is costing the organization and the feasibility of solving it, at the same time keeping the technical issues in perspective, while assuming that technology is bound to feature in the solution. The methodology has four major stages:

1 workflow assessment, whereby an understanding of their client's business and its objectives is obtained;
2 workflow redesign, where a chosen business area is examined to determine how technology could be applied to design a new or changed process;
3 design of the solution, where both technical and business aspects are determined and the technical architecture is set in place;
4 implementation, where the working business system is delivered.

Again this is of significance in that the focus is on information and process rather than on data and entities.

ASPect design method

The ASPect design method is used by Imago Consultants Ltd, a company founded by ex-IBM employees in 1991. They look at nine different stages of considering a process in order to arrive at the specification of a practical workflow and document image processing (DIP) system. Again the methodology is based on the actual business process. The stages which they consider are:

● objectives and priorities;

- the activities involved;
- the information requirements;
- the data format and source;
- work management;
- routeing rules;
- organizational issues;
- management information requirements:
- the operational environment.

Critical success factors

In the context of IM the concept of the critical success factor (CSF) is usually associated with two main areas, the business aims and any system that might support the objectives of the organization.

A CSF is a factor which, if not satisfied, prevents the organization's success. Put another way, the CSFs have to be met for the organization to succeed. Identification of such elements allows management to focus attention on subjects of crucial importance and to prioritize effort and expenditure accordingly. An example of this which has been recognized by many organizations in the last few years is that of customer service – giving the customers what they really want rather than what the company thinks they need. Customer service is then broken down into what it constitutes, such as answering all telephones within four rings, or responding to queries within 24 hours.

The CSF technique is best used where the senior management of an organization are perfectly clear about the aims and objectives of the business, and are keen to identify the information required to support them. CSFs are useful in focusing attention on what is important information and prevent the analysis getting embroiled in a mass of detail.

Use of CSFs in relation to information can be described as identifying those elements of information which must be present to enable the organization to be recognized as achieving its objectives. These are closely linked to the overall business CSFs and, indeed, should support them.

Ray Abi, in his book *Workflow Automation: The New Competitive Edge* (1993), describes a method using factors (systems or information) which directly contribute to the CSFs of the business or 'mission critical systems' and compares these with the CSFs a new system would provide. A matrix of the most important systems versus the CSFs are then scored from one to ten, the system with the highest score being the best target. This method would appear to be rather subjective in the scoring aspects, but may help support a more intuitive selection.

Information audits

A helpful start in getting your information into good order is first to discover what information you have at your disposal by means of an information audit or survey. The general approach is one of considering the department concerned as a factory which takes in raw information and adds value to produce an information product. The information itself is listed together with the way in which value is added and other characteristics such as content, form, format, media, ownership and use. This provides a basis for rationalizing currently available information, identifying information shortfalls and identifying opportunities for exploiting tradeable information.

This can be a laborious and costly exercise, achieved by a combination of questionnaires and interviews, but there are some short cuts. Any personal data currently held on computer, and soon all personal data, is subject to the Data Protection Act and must be registered with the Registrar. Other computerized information is listed in system documentation. Reference to manual information is usually to be found buried within procedure manuals, and sometimes is contained within standard forms.

Activity-based costing

The concept behind activity-based costing (ABC) is that costing should be part of the profit-making process of the business, not just a financial system used by accountants. The idea is that costs should be planned for and managed before they occur rather than monitored and controlled after the event, which is sometimes too late anyway because the commitment to spend the money has already been made.

The traditional method of allocating overhead costs back to operating cost centres has resulted in line managers being faced with centrally incurred costs over which they have no direct control. More attention has been focused on the allocation method as opposed to managing the underlying costs. Activity-based costing concentrates on analysing the activities related to information for the purpose of decision-making, so that managers can understand what drives costs and thus be in a position to manage them better.

Activity-based costing is a tool which can cause significant change within an organization by addressing the real reasons how and why costs are incurred. Effectively it is traditional cost accounting but with a process focus. Rather than identifying the costs involved with a department or function, it identifies the costs associated with provision of a service or product with the relevant service or product.

Strategic cost management

In common with most major accountancy firms, the international firm of Touche Ross (Deloitte Touche Tohmatsu International – DTTI) has developed its own strategic cost management (SCM) methodology, based on ABC methodology. It includes all the aspects of ABC, but provides additionally:

- profitability reporting;
- user-defined attribute analyses, e.g. value added or non-value added, quality related, core or non-core;
- performance measurement;
- data download and manipulation facilities;
- graphical presentation output.

SCM is designed to analyse an entire organization and to present cost, *69* profitability and non-financial data in such a way as to facilitate reviewing operations and making decisions on future business direction.

Both of the last two methods listed above can apply economic or surrogate economic factors to assign value to information. The value of these methods lies in the facilities which they provide to help the explanation of information value and importance, though of course this is not their principal or original purpose.

Return on investment

Another tool used by Touche Ross to assist their clients is known as renewing organizational infrastructure (ROI). This is actually a tool-kit of over 30 individual tools to analyse the organization in terms of activities, processes, structure, customer requirements, outputs, drivers, inputs and performance measures.

The tools provide a means to:

● determine processes and activities;
● determine activity headcounts;
● produce a product and activity map;
● overlay unit costs and skills;
● determine the costs drivers.

Culture print

Change management is a vital aspect of implementing systems which dramatically change the way your organization works. Some perfectly satisfactory systems have failed because they have not been accepted by those who will use them. Change management is a large subject warranting entire books on the topic. Here, I will cover a methodology which provides some structure to manage an intuitive and delicate process, that of persuading people to change.

Culture print is based on analysing the nature of such an intangible as the internal culture of an organization. The methodology, in common with others, suggests three levels of culture within an organization:

1　*The most visible level of physical manifestations.* These are usually identified as the organizational structure, the policies and procedures, and the reward criteria.
2　*The values and attitudes of staff.* These are reflected in the perceptions of individuals, the way in which values are demonstrated in practice, and what symbols are used to convey values.
3　*The basic assumptions.* These are invisible and underly the entire ethos of the organization. They are usually taken for granted and largely implicit.

The methodology consists of six steps which result in a profile of the culture which can be used as a starting point in deciding how best to implement change:

1 *Establishment of project parameters*. This includes agreeing objectives, clarifying expectations and identifying major strategic and organizational issues.
2 *Information gathering*. This consists of capturing information about the present culture by means of questionnaires, staff interviews, workshops and executive interviews.
3 *Analysis*. The information obtained is reviewed and graphical outputs compiled. Key issues are probed.
4 *Feedback*. The findings are presented and workshops held to explore possible implications for change.
5 *Implications for change*. Here the traits of the organization are identified, together with what it means for change. For example, a trait of lack of teamwork implies that change is unlikely to be driven successfully by teams, therefore change agents should be used. Similarly, a high focus and agreement on external issues such as customer awareness will facilitate change. The best approach is designed and implemented.
6 *Benchmarking*. The process of change is monitored through the transition stage and fine-tuned if necessary. As change is a never-ending process, so the monitoring should be repeated at regular intervals.

Information will be one of the categories towards which attitudes and cultural behaviours of staff are assessed.

Cost and value analysis

This method, first proposed by Best (1984) and developed by Horton, is referred to in Chapter 2. While it is usually quite straightforward to discover the cost of information, it is very difficult to be prescriptive about its value. A piece of information has a different value depending on the recipient's point of view and timing can be crucial. This has an interesting impact on the relative importance of immediacy and accuracy. Sometimes in crucial business decisions, it is better to have 'ball-park figures' immediately than wait for accurate figures which could take hours or even days to compute.

To assist managers in planning, monitoring and controlling their information resources, the Management Systems and Efficiency division of HM Treasury produced a methodology 'the cost and value of information' (CVI) which consisted of eight steps and which concentrated on the external outputs from a department in relation to:

1 Define objectives and decide selection criteria.
2 Identify information outputs, select information items.
3 Describe information items.
4 Perform customer value survey.
5 Calculate production costs.
6 Analyse findings.
7 Develop solution and test it.
8 Implementation plan.

Having identified the information outputs, the costs of producing each of the chosen items is determined and its value established. As mentioned above, information has a different value in different circumstances, so rather than specifying a cash value, the value is assessed in terms of the use to which it is applied and how it helps staff in their work. It is then possible to highlight high-cost, low-value items and determine an appropriate course of action.

Total quality management (TQM)

A total quality approach to managing an organization requires all members of that organization to accept that there is only one priority in business: meeting customer requirements efficiently and effectively. This means that staff should develop a comprehensive understanding of their role in the business process. This would involve openly discussing problems in order to improve performance and objectivity in exploring with colleagues the underlying reasons for the problems. Thus an open supportive culture is established, which aims to overcome problems jointly and seeks to achieve ever more demanding performance targets.

The TQM approach differs from conventional management approaches in that the discussion of problems is actively encouraged. Staff who solve problems are more highly motivated as a result. This opposes the tendency in some organizations to treat problems negatively, taking a disciplinary approach to improvement by publicizing errors that are usually outside staff control. Another aspect is the inclination to provide quick fixes to problems as opposed to a more thorough, longer-term solution, engendering the culture that 'that will do'. With TQM, the culture of 'best in class' is encouraged, so that there is continual striving for improvement.

TQM has been proven in certain service industries to reduce significantly the costs of waste activities, such as error correction, which can contribute 15 to 40 per cent of operating costs. TQM is also effective in identifying the ineffectiveness of existing management initiatives. The focus on customer satisfaction matches closely the BPR approach of analysing a process from the customer viewpoint.

Success in implementing a TQM programme comes from determination to improve quality, from the chief executive down, by changing the culture of the organization. This can only be achieved by education and training, planning a programme of activities which deliver improvements and reinforcing success.

PROCESS MODELLING TOOLS

Why model?

Every organization has a number of processes which it carries out in order to achieve its business objectives. An understanding of these forms the basis for designing a new process, re-engineering a current process or applying technology to support the process. A model is a way of analysing and recording the process and forms the basis for discussion between different parties. A picture speaks a thousand words and with graphical models it is easier to highlight shortfalls, problems and to try 'what ifs'.

A model should be a good communication medium, able to be easily interpreted by all involved in the exercise. As many IM and BPR projects are now user led and the tools have to be easy to use, a graphical model fits the bill.

As I have said before, no tool alone will redesign your business for you, you still need skilled analysts. Also it is important to involve users to obtain first-hand knowledge of what actually happens in practice. It is difficult to find users in most traditional hierarchical organizations who have a detailed view of the whole process. Managers may understand the whole process but only have an overview of what goes on. Departmental staff are usually expert in their own domain, but know little of what happens to information before it enters and after it leaves their territory.

There are several different reasons why an organization may be considering the use of modelling tools, some of which are shown below:

- to document current procedures, possibly as part of implementing a quality system, or as a means to communicate the procedures to staff. This could include the use of the tool merely as a presentation medium;
- in order to understand a current process;
- as a basis for redesigning a current process;
- to design a new process;
- in order to apply TQM techniques to improve a process;
- to support a process with a computer system, or perhaps as the first step towards generating a workflow system.

All of the above reasons require the modelling tool to provide a sound understanding of the process in a way that can be communicated easily. There several different types of tools and within each type several different examples, so what is important in the process modelling tool's notation and how it is used in the model? Martyn Ould (1993) of Praxis states eight laws for process modelling:

1 If you must have abstractions, then make them concrete abstractions. Any process modelling notation must deal in concepts which people can relate to, otherwise how can they tell if a model is right?
2 The real world is messy. The notation must be able to model messes when necessary. Muddle modelling is the norm, not the exception.
3 A model must mean something and only one thing. If your model is ambiguous, how can you tell what it is telling you?
4 Process models are about people, and for people. The notation must make sense to people. If you cannot explain it in ten minutes, it does not make sense.
5 There is what people actually do and there is what they effectively do. These are different and we must be able to model both.
6 People do processes, but they work in functions. These two mess each other up. A model must capture both – and the conflict between them.

7   It is what people produce as outputs, not what they do to data, that counts. A process is about doing, deciding and co-operating. It is not about data.
8   There are some basic business patterns like the case, the plan, the delegate-report pair, the periodical report cycle and the contract. We want to be able to capture them in our models.

Diagramming features

Virtually all process modelling tools have a strong emphasis on the way they represent a process graphically. At one end of the scale are tools which do little more than provide an electronic means to draw a flowchart, such as WorkDraw, which is fine if that is all you want to do. At the other end of the scale are tools which can take the information created at the process modelling stage, run animated simulations and then effectively generate the live system, usually by linking to another associated tool. An example of this is Oracle Process Modeller.

Derek Miers(1993) of Enix Ltd, describes six basic categories of diagramming techniques in *Process Product Watch*, which I have outlined below together with some views on their attributes:

1   *Hierarchical.* This is the approach of building decomposition diagrams using tree diagrams to break down the subject which is being analysed, as in Enterprise Modeller. This can be applied to the functional hierarchy, the process itself, data and materials used and it enables the view of only a single dimension of the subject, which can be effective if drill-down or related decompositions can be viewed subsequently.
2   *Flow diagrams.* Virtually every tool contains the concept of flow to show the sequence of events within a process. Without additional information, this is about all it does show. Some tools allow role information to be added to the basic flow, such as EIR and ProcessWise Workbench, while others have interfaces between process definitions and the flow diagrams. Flow diagrams are useful because the graphic representation of the process allows easier identification of anomalies such as streams which go nowhere.
3   *IDEF (ICAM definition model; ICAM is 'integrated computer-aided manufacturing')* is a modelling standard developed by the US Department of Defense to provide a formal and rigorous set of semantics for describing systems. In this approach, activities are represented as boxes and the forces which work upon them, such as inputs, outputs and controls, as arrows. Activities can be decomposed and text associated with each diagram. This is a rigorous standard which may be useful for the expert to use in modelling complex processes, but is less likely to be effective in the hands of the business user. *IDEF3* is a development of IDEF, intended as a mechanism to speed up the process of describing business systems. It consists of a tool to provide a scenario, in terms of the steps in a process and what the process is concerned with. There is also a means to capture the dynamics of the process.
4   *Role activity diagrams (RADs)* concentrate on the roles and activities

constituting a process, interactions between those roles, the business rules which apply and the information associated with the process. Roles carry out activities in a particular sequence, so RADs are effectively flow diagrams with inherent information on responsibilities. The use of roles as opposed to job titles enables the process to be analysed logically rather than physically, which presents opportunities for reorganization. This technique is advantageous when modelling is being used to document, improve or redesign a process.

5   *Action workflow diagrams* are of a diagrammatic style based on linguistics and the network of commitments that people make with one another. The concept is based around a 'Workflow elliptical loop', representing the four phases of activity in any human interaction: preparation, negotiation, performance and acceptance. The two parties concerned are the 'customer' and the 'performer'. This technique allows the subjects people talk about to be represented.

6   *Systems thinking.* Within systems thinking, a process is a sequence of activities through which material flows in order to have value added to it. The three main elements are stocks, flow and feedback links. A fourth element known as a converter is used to represent a goal or constant in the calculations. This approach is useful in understanding the behaviour of the business and how one part of the process affects others. Systems thinking is a graphical simulation language as opposed to a graphical process description tool.

Another feature of modelling tools is the ability to attach workload information or process measures such as the time, cost or effort involved in performing a particular task within a process. This generally leads on to facilities to animate the workflow, by varying different parameters and observing the effect on loads and bottlenecks, as in Witness.

Simulation features

Simulations can be provided by two fundamentally different approaches. Traditional modelling tools, such as decision support systems, are based on the rules of statistical probability, using forecasting techniques and queuing theory. The simulation effect is achieved by underlying algorithms or formulas which have been designed to behave like the real world, showing the results based on a particular set of variables. These are sometimes known as 'What if?' simulations or static simulations since there is no concept of the time element. The spreadsheet is a simple form of this sort of tool, showing static results for each combination of the variables in the form of pie charts, graphs or matrices of data.

The other type of simulation found in some process modelling tools is known as dynamic modelling, where the concept of time is involved. Within dynamic modelling, there are two techniques which can be applied:

1   *Discrete event simulation* involves dividing a process up into discrete elements which have time and resource associated with them. Events are

modelled as beginning at one point in time and completing at another, effectively driven by the calendar, and peaks and troughs or waiting times are demonstrated. Most process simulation tools use this approach.

2 *Time slice simulation* takes a snapshot of the process at regular time intervals, showing the state of the process at that point in time. When the snapshots are put together, a general view of the process is obtained, giving an average performance as opposed to identifying peaks and troughs.

Other facilities include a means of interfacing with external products, for downloading information for presentation or analysis of data. Another feature is that of an ABC facility, where the activity is broken down into elements which can be accurately timed and hence costed. In BPR terms, this means that the case for redesigning a process can be supported by hard benefits.

Summary of process modelling tools available

In Table 4.1 I have taken some of the features of process modelling tools and indicated to which products they apply. Diagramming techniques are discussed above. Work measures include the capture of information of time, effort, cost, the frequency of the operation, value-added attribute and even user-defined measures. A 'Yes' in this box indicates that the product offers at least one of the measures. 'What if' simulation means that the product itself is able to provide some form of simulation. Animation means that the tool can demonstrate the simulation using screen animation techniques, so that the process appears to run before your very eyes. The system generation column indicates whether the tool itself, following the modelling of the process, can be used to establish the basis of the operational system, removing the need to transcribe the information gathered during the modelling process.

Table 4.1   Summary of Process Modelling Tools

Product	Diagramming Techniques	Work Measures	'What if' Simulations	System Generation
ActionWorkflow Analyst*	ActionWorkflow	No	No	Yes, with Action Workflow Builder
Business Design Facility (BDF)*	Flow, Decomposition, IDEF	Yes	No, but interface facility	No, but interface facility
Business Intelligence facility (BIF)#`	Flow, Decomposition	Some	No, but interfaces with ProcessWise Workbench	No, but interfaces with ProcessWise Integrator

Product	Diagramming Techniques	Work Measures	'What if' Simulations	System Generation
CASEwise Modeller	Flow, Decomposition	Yes	Yes, time slice	Yes, for traditional IT systems
EIR	Flow Decomposition	Yes	No	Yes, for traditional IT systems
Enterprise Modeller	Flow, Decomposition, IDEF	Yes	No, but interface facility	No
IDEF	IDEF	Yes	No, but file download	No
IThink	Flow, Systems thinking	Yes	Yes, time slice	No
Oracle Process Modeller	Flow	Yes	Yes, animation	Yes, with Oracle CDE2 CASE
ProcessWise Workbench	Flow, IDEF, Decomposition	Yes	Yes	Yes, ProcessWise Integrator
Quesheet	Decomposition	Yes, deduced	Yes	No
RADitor	RAD	No	No	No
SES/workbench	Flow	Yes	Yes, animation	No
TOP-IX	Flow	Yes	Yes	No
Witness	Flow	Yes	Yes, discrete event animation	No
WorkDraw	Flow	Yes	No, but interface facility	No

* indicates that the tool addresses information
\# indicates that the tool addresses information and data
no mark indicates that the tool analyses data elements only

The table is not intended to be a comprehensive list of products available on the market today. A good source of information on the latest tools and their features can be found in *Process Product Watch*, published by Enix Ltd. Contact numbers for the above mentioned tools can be found in the contacts list in the Appendix.

Configuration management tools

When purchasing a turnkey system from a supplier, the second most important issue after functionality is that of performance. Most suppliers provide a configuration model which takes the clients' estimates of the volumes of scanned input, retrievals and workflow transactions, together with the hardware platform and software proposed, in order to confirm the whole system will work to satisfactory performance levels. Both normal loading and peak loading should be demonstrated.

Most of these tools are spreadsheet models which simulate the operation of the system, so are not 100 per cent accurate. However, they should give some level of comfort about system performance. There are other techniques which may provide more accurate statistics and hence prevent embarrassment when the system is first implemented:

- Perform a volume test, based on the live software, hardware and network, just prior to implementation, together with data specifically designed to reflect the live business transactions under peak conditions. This is an expensive test to design and mount, but should give the closest approximation to live running.
- Ask the supplier to identify one of their current clients with a similar system in terms of software and volume. This will give some indication of the capacity required but there will be numerous small differences which might compound into giving a misleading result.
- Utilize third party facilities, such as Sequent Computer Systems Ltd's 'Wall of Windows' (see Appendix), and test its performance running on a range of hardware. This would provide an independent view of performance in an interactive, real-time environment.

REFERENCES

Abi, R. (1993), *Workflow Automation: The New Competitive Edge*, Stamford, CT: Unitech International Corporation. (Available from AIIM in US.)

Best, D.P. (1984), 'Information Mapping', in B. Cronin, *Information Management from Strategy to Action,* London: ASLIB.

Burk, C.F. and Horton, F.W. (1988), *Infomap: A Complete Guide to Discovering Corporate Information Resources*, Englewood Cliffs, NJ: Prentice Hall.

Checkland, P. (1984), *Systems Thinking, Systems Practice*, Chichester: John Wiley.

CCTA (1990), *Managing Information as a Resource*, London: HMSO.

Horton, F.W. (1994), 'Infomapper Revisited', *Aslib Proceedings*, **46** (4), 117–20.

Irving, P. (1993), 'Integrating Technology into the Business', Document 93,

Conference Proceedings, Blenheim Online, Blenheim House, 630 Chiswick High Road, London W4 5BG.

Kay, M. H. (1993), 'Document Content Management – Towards an Object Oriented Approach'. Document 93, Conference Proceedings, Blenheim Online, Blenheim House, 630 Chiswick High Road, London W4 5BG.

Mabberley, J. (1992), *Activity-Based Costing in Financial Institutions*, London: Pitman.

Miers, D. (1993), *Process Product Watch*, Richmond, Surrey: Enix Limited.

Ould, M. (1993), 'Eight Laws for Process Modelling', *IOPener*, **2** (4), Bath: Praxis plc.

Modelling Business Processes, Bath: Praxis plc.

Touche Ross Management Consultants (1994), *Information Management: A Survey of Current Practices and Trends – 1994*, London: Touche Ross Management Consultants.

5 Managing the fourth resource
Bill Thom

The technologies referred to in this book have included a range of advances which have been recognized in retrospect as key technologies. In this chapter Bill Thom, one of the pioneers of text retrieval and now with one of the most techno- logically advanced of the document management technology companies, Interleaf, takes us through some of these. He covers the key technology events and describes the role which these have played in moving us to the position where IM as it has been described in the preceding chapters can become reality.

One aspect is document management, the means whereby the creation, stor- age, retrieval and manipulation of documents through their life cycle is achieved. Bill explains the impact of each of these in a way which conveys vividly how the information revolution is being moved forward by these technological develop- ments, concluding with examples of hypertext to show how one technology can assist in the addition of value to our information sources.

The organization of information has been a matter of concern since papyrus scrolls were created and stored in Greece in the great library in Alexandria. The earliest use of full text indexing can be traced back to the fourteenth century when Cistercian monks created the first biblical concordance. However, it was not until the invention of the printing press that we eventually saw large-scale book production which in turn gave rise to libraries of books and all the issues involved in managing major document collections.

Until the late 1960s the skills of document management resided in a range of related professional specialists – librarians, information scientists and archivists. But around this time, a new force emerged quietly on to the infor- mation scene. Information technology (IT), founded on the use of computers for information management, began what some have predicted is a new infor- mation revolution.[1] To the recognised resources of production – people, raw materials and machinery – we have added a new dimension. Information is the fourth resource and document management is one of the main means by which we can exploit it.

The purpose of this chapter is to consider the management of the fourth resource, and to look at how information storage, retrieval and distribution are at the centre of the information revolution.

The legacy

There is a vast legacy of information in the world in the form of books, reports, journal articles, newspaper stories, minutes, proceedings, theses, patents, standards, case histories and so on. Our collective knowledge as a society is bound up in these records and documents. It forms most of the base of our education in universities and colleges and it provides the great repositories to which current thinkers and philosophers of our own time can continue to add to the complex web of human understanding.

Through the 1970s and right up to today, the volume of information has extended greatly beyond the traditional communication medium of print. In a modern school, college or university, the learning process incorporates all forms of resources, for instance – video films, broadcasts, audio-tapes, illustrations, databases, photographs. We have even invented a new information vocabulary – data highways, multimedia, information warehouses, artificial intelligence, expert systems and virtual reality – which conjure up images of the new information age. But when we see the pace of change accelerate with each new technological breakthrough, we are prone to question why we should be doing all this. 'Where are we going?' you may have asked, and 'Where is it all going to end?' Can the vision of Bill Gates, the president of Microsoft, and the technospeak of his generation sit comfortably alongside, and add value to, the legacy left to us by the scholars and intellectuals of the age of print?'

With all the hype, and the haste surrounding IT, the world of business seems hard pressed to capitalize on the new possibilities presented by the technology, and there seems to be far less time today to absorb the effects of one raft of changes before the next wave of opportunities confront us. The world of instant communication seems to bring with it the corresponding threat of increasingly rapid obsolescence. But making economic sense of information management and its potential effects on business and business processes is becoming one of the most critical management issues of the day. To take one simple example, just consider how rapidly we have changed the way in which documents are created.

Short time passing . . .

What have they done with all the typewriters? They generated between them most of the printed material in the world and how quickly they have disappeared – replaced by the dedicated word processor which itself was quickly made obsolete by the personal computer.

One of the major problems in information management has been the difficulty of capturing data, especially text, in electronic re-usable form. Today we are close to solving that problem and by 1996, according to the Gartner Group[2] we shall reach the halfway milestone when more than 50 per cent of the office information in business will be captured electronically. Once we learn to harvest this information base we will be able to move further along the path to perhaps the ultimate goal of the new information age – any information, any time, anywhere. What has brought this event nearer?

THE CONDITIONS FOR A REVOLUTION

According to Karl Marx, social revolution cannot occur until all the conditions for it to happen are in place.[3] The 'advances' described below are generally regarded as the key technologies which the market has identified as the necessary foundations on which to build an information revolution. Are these part of a grand master-plan? Is there a great design and a road-map – or are we simply seeing opportunism at work, driven by the perceived needs of a volatile market? Planned, or with us by accident, these fundamental prerequisites for the new information age are now largely in place.

The information technology components of the new information age

- The invention of the large mainframe computer – made famous by IBM and acting as the first information repositories. (Despite recent downturns, IBM mainframes and Amdahl systems still hold most of the world's large legacy collections of information and most huge dial-up information databases.)
- The invention of the minicomputer largely attributed to DEC which grew out of the need for small computers to put into outer space (most likely today to be a Unix machine rather than a proprietary operating system).
- The word processor, which appeared first as special hardware and then quickly disappeared to be embodied in personal computer software for word processing, and desktop publishing (the way almost all documents are created initially).
- The personal computer – attributed to IBM (and now cloned by everyone else).
- The development of the computer network and the linking of personal computers and workstations to a central machine
- The development of the local area network, linking individual groups of personal computers together, often with a minicomputer as a shared repository (slow to catch on at first but now a massive growth area).
- The development of the wide area network via satellite or landline, linking users in one network with information stored on a remote machine or with users on that network (and now forming the basis on which we can all join the data highway).
- The creation of the optical storage device capable of mass storage of text and document images (portable on-line libraries).
- The creation of document scanning technology (electronic microfilm).
- The invention of the CD-ROM. (Compact Read-Only technology may become the dominant distribution medium for all information and documents for a wide audience.)

- The invention of optical character recognition, and intelligent character recognition (For converting older and incoming documents into a medium which can be 'understood' and indexed by computers).

- The invention of the optical 'juke box' for storing vast image and document libraries (the replacement of the office filing cabinets, and possibly the libraries).

- The emergence of the relational database (making separation of data and program a reality and making classes of information 'stored once' re-usable in many applications).

- The creation of client-server computing (separation of the interface from the central information repository encouraging shared data and collaboration).

- The evolution of massively parallel processing (where many thousands of processors can act in parallel to process vast volumes of information in fractions of a second).

- The invention of text retrieval and its gradual acceptance over many years (opening up the potential for content-based searching of unstructured information – the key to unlocking the value of documents).

- The creation of electronic mail systems (providing much more than messages between people; also a transport layer for moving information around efficiently).

- The creation of electronic workflow and document routing (removing the need for serial processing of documents and freeing us from the wait-states which reliance on paper imposes).

- The creation of electronic document viewing technology (the means by which we could eliminate paper from the equation much of the time).

- The emergence of UNIX and Windows NT (possibly the nearest we shall ever get to a universal operating system).

- The emergence and domination of Microsoft and Windows 3 as a generic PC-based user interface (which has made the use of computers possible for masses of ordinary workers).

- The invention of object databases and document markup standards. (The vast size of the document opportunity requires new methods and new concepts. As more and more information becomes available on the data highway there will be a need for more standards to make objects share-able, that is, SGML (standard generalized markup language, CCITT/4 (International Consultative Committee on Telegraphy and Telephony), IGES (Initial Graphics Exchange Specification) JPEG (Joint Photographic Exchange Group) and MPEG (Moving Picture Exchange Group)).

- Speech recognition technology (to make data input just a matter of speaking into a machine – the end of the keyboard eventually).

The real value is in the information – not the technology

Despite these many technology breakthroughs, it still takes time to fully realize their potential and the process of change is just as problematic in IT as it is elsewhere. One of the hardest notions to accept today is the speed with which the technology we are using will become obsolete. Though we are driven to spend large sums of money on hardware such as diskstores, terminals, work-stations and even central computers, it is important to understand that they are disposable tools. What we are really investing in is the *information we put into these systems.* The information persists, and if we are to benefit from it, we need to protect it. It is our fourth resource and worth far more than the technology. Raw information by itself is worthless, but brought together and organized, rallied into rational argument, pointed at specific problems, it becomes knowledge. It is often said that information is power, but that cliché is a simplification. It is access to information and the ability to know how and when to apply it that brings us power.

Technology as the means to harness information

Most organizations are now beginning to realize the importance of information and how essential it is to invest in it. In some industries, where the information itself is the 'product' this has always been evident, but investment even in the following sectors has been patchy:

- newspapers;
- publishing;
- on-line database vending;
- broadcasting;
- legal industry.

In another range of organizations, information is so closely associated with the 'product' that it has a clearly perceived value:

- financial services;
- software product manufacturers;
- most government departments;
- most scientific research centres.

We now have another set of industries which are becoming highly regulated by the government and its agents where information has a critical role to play in the continued existence of the industry. This may be due to environmental factors, safety, quality, product liability and the like:

- pharmaceutical industry;
- petrochemical industry;
- nuclear industry;
- construction industry;
- electricity and water industries.

Across a wide range of manufacturing industry there is a similar push towards information management. Driven by the issues of quality and the increasing need for competitive edge, we are witnessing sizeable investments in document management by the following:

- aircraft manufacturers;
- automotive manufacturers;
- defence-related industries;
- ancillary and components manufacturers (often for the above).

TO BE PROCESSED IT MUST BE CAPTURED

Information must be capable of being processed by the technology and first of all it has to be captured into computers. Manual typewriters and other non-electronic means of creating documents were effectively dead ends, that is, you could not easily read the output into a computer system.

While most of today's information is generated electronically (directly in a re-usable form) the business world still reverts very often to the printer and the photocopying machine to use the information. Gradually this is changing, and many organizations are beginning to remove the use of paper from many areas of work. Why are they doing this?

Paper-based systems create their own particular problems and for the most part, the flow of work in a paper system is severely restricted by the nature of the medium itself. In business processes where decisions are progressed through step-by-step forwarding of documents, the slow and cumbersome passage of paper dictates the pace of work. Manual mailing of documents between people is fundamentally inefficient, since the documents spend most time in transit or waiting for us to do something with them at our convenience. In addition, one document in a pile arriving in your physical mail receives no particular priority and it is difficult to separate the 'wheat from the chaff'. Finally, when human beings are part of the chain, the flow will tend to break down completely whenever individuals are away from their desks, for example at meetings, out on business trips, on vacations or off sick. The potential market for electronic workflow and document management to overcome many of these problems is far greater than most people realize. It could be hundreds of times larger than the traditional market for computing which has tended to concentrate on database applications. Databases are used for only 5 per cent of our information, the remaining 95 per cent is mainly in the form of documents.

Changing this is of course rather difficult in traditional environments where the drive to cut cost is not felt quite so acutely. For example the Civil Service may still rely for some time on the signed and well-drafted memorandum passed through the hierarchy. In other sectors, however, the attack on paper is an unstoppable movement driven by the massive expenditure committed to printing and distribution of documents of all kinds.

Scanning and character recognition

The volume of printed and paper-based legacy information can only be captured into the new order through the process known as scanning. A scanner creates an electronic image of each page of a document which is more or less like a photograph. This electronic representation is being introduced increasingly to remove paper from the business process.

Document image processing is a fast growing application market. Combined with workflow technology, this gives a powerful solution to the routine paper-based processes which clog up offices and administration. Workflow is the means to bring all the resources needed to carry out the job to the desktop workstation. Here the document is an image, and it is delivered via e-mail. It will be prioritized subject to rules and action will be expected by a certain time which is logged by the system. If the job is not carried out there will be an alert or an escalation procedure and the emphasis will be to increase throughput and get rid of the inertia caused by physical paper passing.

Although an image of a document will occupy far more storage space on the disk storage than would a file keyboarded into a word processing system, it has obvious advantages. It can deal with graphics and multiple languages, hieroglyphics, handwriting and any other marks on the paper. It can be sent in a few seconds. It can be controlled and filed centrally in a database. It can be restricted only to those who need to see it. It can be indexed and archived properly – just once. It can be forwarded to others by e-mail or by fax. Finally, it can be printed from the system back on to paper.

Various document imaging system suppliers have developed numerous applications for this technology from archiving and retrieval of the paper at the simple level, through to complex paperless office processes involving the electronic movement of documents across a company, between offices or even between continents. A comprehensive review of this technology and its benefits is available from the Delphi Consulting Group.[4]

Retrieval and storage of simple images of documents such as council tax forms, insurance claims or purchase orders provide few headaches. The system usually incorporates a database and this provides basic attribute retrieval on account number, client name, part number etc.

For more complex documents where there is narrative content such as reports, detailed correspondence, background papers, journal articles and so forth, there may be a need to convert the contents of the document into something that can be read by computer systems. The method used to recognize text in this way is known as optical character recognition (OCR). Many projects which require to capture older documents rely heavily on character recognition and, properly qualified, OCR can be an extremely productive and cost-effective method by which to achieve data capture. However, it is an inexact process depending heavily on the quality of the original printed document, the typeface and the kind of paper, and numerous techniques have been developed to eliminate the potentially high number of misreads which OCR delivers. ICR, (intelligent character recognition) improves the situation but in general, despite year-on-year improvements in the technology, its usage is still problematic. A review of the latest techniques involved is contained in a special issue of a journal called *Electronic Documents*.[5] Where necessary, if OCR/ICR fails, the only alternative is to re-key the original documents.

INFORMATION RETRIEVAL

With an increasingly vast repository of corporate information becoming available in machine readable form, how can the value tied up in this huge document storehouse be realized. The answer to this problem lies in the fundamental enabling technology behind the information revolution, generally termed *information retrieval.*

Librarians devised practical methods by which to classify the books on their shelves typified by the Dewey Decimal system used in most public libraries. This and other variations such as the Universal Decimal Classification and other schemes provided a way to organize a collection of physical document objects on shelves, bringing like subjects together. Such systems were sufficient for the information browser prepared to search through the collection. The more sophisticated user would approach the library catalogue, a large collection of surrogate information organized into a card catalogue providing both subject and author access to the complete contents of the library. This meta-data was used for searching instead of searching through the document collection itself.

While this type of information retrieval is still prominent for the general purpose enquiry, today the complete text or abstracts of the documents are available for on-line searching. Services such as Knight Rider, Mead Data Services, FT Profile, Reuters etc. assist a vast community of business subscribers who dial in to search the very large on-line databases which are effectively full-text libraries. Newspapers, patents, journal articles, financial information and many other sources are captured and made available for a fee. In these services, full-text searching is supported by high-speed indexing systems. Typically the user specifies search terms of interest; the system reports back a list of 'hits' which qualify, and the user selectively views a range of these documents.

The retrieval methods used in this type of solution are now becoming widely used in many other text- and document-based applications appearing as an option in document management, office systems, specialist CD-ROM publications and collections, and in many thousands of in-house text-based applications. The searching technology itself has a wide range of functions and many competing products based on varying approaches. John Ashford and Peter Willetts have covered most of these in an easy-to-digest book on the subject[6] and a more recent paper outlines some of the latest methodology.[7]

In view of the crucial nature of the text retrieval process to the successful use of the new information resources, we should examine it more critically.

Natural language versus controlled language

There is a debate on the best method for searching text which has been in the background of the information professions for many years and continues to the present time.

For many involved in the debate, full-text searching seemed to pose a threat since librarians and information specialists were inclined to the view that in order to find information, you first had to classify, catalogue and index it. To achieve this, the language used in documents in a particular subject domain had to be analysed and a subject thesaurus developed. This latter tool was effectively a standard artificial language which was used to define approved keywords to be applied to all the documents being added to the collection.

This 'added value' provided a means to achieve consistent search results across a database irrespective of the particular terms used by individual searchers. Basically the terms used by searchers were automatically converted to the meta-language of the thesaurus. This became the 'controlled language' school which defended the need to employ skilled information professionals to convert the contents of documents into true meaning, that is, the terms approved in the thesaurus.

The other school of thought, those in favour of natural language searching, held that if authors could be relied upon to produce documents, the terms they used in their documents were themselves sufficient as keywords for searching. At a simplistic level, this approach appeared quite compelling since computers could ostensibly carry out the indexing and avoid all the delay and cost in using professional people.

It is not our purpose here to promote the case for one or other of these approaches except to say that there seems to be merit in sensible application of both in different circumstances. In subjects where the terminology is well defined, perhaps natural language is good enough. However, in some subject areas, where the language is loose, where there is constant change and new terminology leads to confusion, a degree of applied language control may be very beneficial or even essential.

In many organizations economics tends to have settled the issue irrespective of merit since controlling language, indexing and other manpower intensive activities have been cut back or eliminated. The problem at the end of the day comes down to probability. Statistically, in any collection of documents, only a small percentage of the items (perhaps as low as 25 per cent) of the items of information will be used to answer the bulk of the enquiries (more than 75 per cent) made of it. If we could predict in advance which items were going to be in the 25 per cent (that is, make a value judgement about the potential value and use of each document), then we could probably afford to index these any way we wanted.

This takes us to the crux of the matter. 'Why should there not be a value judgement?' The vast repositories of textual information are fine in theory, but they do nothing about deciding which are the *best* papers on a subject. Indeed our whole academic reward system tends to favour those who publish as many articles as possible with scant regard to the quality of contributions.

While the latest text retrieval tools will give you a ranked list of the hits you have retrieved, they will never be able to tell you which of these ranked items are the best or most interesting in terms of contribution to the subject, which are purely repetition of other ideas, and which are simply fillers to make up a publications 'quota'.

Clearly, the larger these databases become, the more acutely we shall suffer from over-retrieval. What is the use of an information warehouse if we must still play at 'hunt the thimble'?

ADDING VALUE

Most of us learn from documents such as books when we are young. We read from left to right and progress in a linear fashion through the content. But this activity is very time-consuming and there is such a vast number of sources to be covered. Something else we learn when we are children is that while we are encouraged to scribble and draw, we are told not to do this on printed books. The printed book therefore takes on a special significance for us as something fixed and frozen. The creators of illustrated manuscripts in the Middle Ages did not suffer from this problem, and if you look at these wonderfully crafted documents, you will often see margin notes, and many additions made over the years as readers made connections between what they were reading and perhaps other thoughts and ideas they came across. Even in modern times, the sacrosanct nature of the book breaks down in universities, where the student will underline and add notes in the margins at will. All of this confirms the need for us to add value to our information sources.

For the collections of documents that can be built up over time, there is a big opportunity for information specialists to add value. The skills of the librarian can now be applied to guiding users through the information in the database, taking them along a discovery trail. Experienced users can also begin to start using databases of documents and create their own connections and trails, adding electronic notes 'in the margin' just like the early creators of illustrated manuscripts. This process is known as hypertext, a concept popularized by Theodore (Ted) Nelson[8] in a literary information project called Xanadu in the early 1980s. It was a scientist by the name of Vannevar Bush, who forecast the concept of hypertext as early as 1942.[9] Bush suggested that the gathering mass of knowledge in scientific papers should be served by an information machine, and using search and storage logic based on the way the human brain works, rather than through formal classification schemes.

Rather than treat a document database as a passive entity, using hypertext we can add great richness to it and begin to exploit the information to the point where we can develop information into knowledge. A more up-to-date review of this concept by MacMorrow and Baird extends the argument to cover multimedia[10] and this whole area is the subject of much current interest to publishers and broadcasters alike.

There is nevertheless a sense of pessimism experienced by many people confronted by these vast information warehouses and the problem of noisy over-retrieval might be tempered by products and services which can turn at least some of it into knowledge. Value judgements are what we need here, to provide us with potential connections between related documents and objects. This is what hypertext delivers, to the extent that users of the database are guided by a network of 'point and click' cross-references, added notes, comments and links to information in other databases. In addition, if we as users can add value ourselves to that process, which some of the latest software tools will allow, then the dialogue between the person and the information warehouse might yet prove to be a voyage of discovery and not of disenchantment.

If we introduce sound, vision and non-linear hypertext navigation, we are starting to exploit the tools of the new information revolution to their full potential. Innovation is often a matter of luck. A coincidence sparks off an idea, a chance encounter with a colleague may create a new and fruitful line of enquiry. While we cannot replace this pure serendipity, if we set about adding value in a methodical way to information collections we might eventually enhance the opportunity for greater innovation. Users can also leave a collection of documents slightly improved by recording their own discoveries every time they use it, leaving in the database a set of new hypertext links for others to follow. Some will argue that to prevent complete anarchy someone has to decide if these new links and paths themselves are of value. Here there will be a continuing role for the information professional needed to ensure the integrity and validity of the database – no longer a passive resource, but almost a living, developing entity. However the task is managed, we shall have done something to perhaps give inspiration to those who follow us on their own quest for knowledge.

An example of hypertext in action

Graphical navigation aids

Graphical navigation aids (GNAs) in the form of buttons and documents can be created to guide users at every step of the way. Figure 5.1 shows a graphical table of contents (TOC) which helps the user visualize how the material in the Brown University Dickens Web collection is organized. Users can click on the hyperlink button beside any topic to access material related to that topic.

An entry in a TOC or a single idea in the text might lead to several related concepts. In the Interleaf implementation of the Brown University Dickens Web collection, each hypertext link in the overview leads to a 'crossroads'

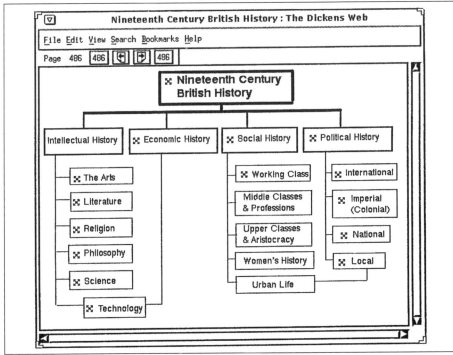

Figure 5.1   Table of contents as a GNA

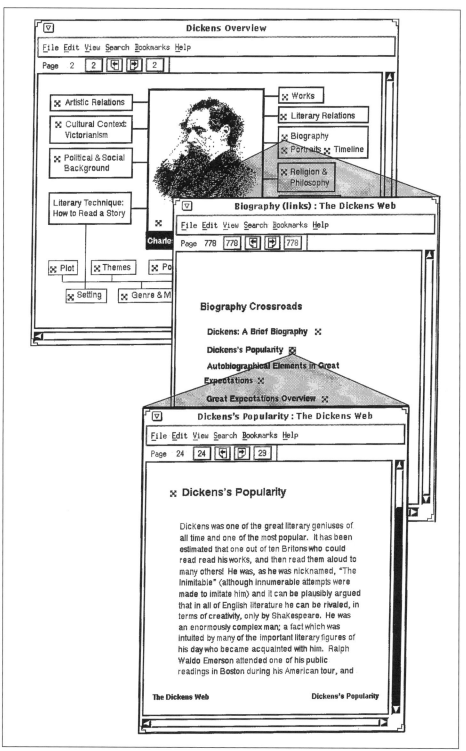

Figure 5.2   Navigating through crossroads documents

document that gives the user a choice of destinations. An example of how 'crossroads' documents help users to navigate through on-line information is shown in Figure 5.2.

POINT AND CLICK DISTRIBUTION

The trouble with printing

Since the appearance of the first printed books and the arrival of Caxton's printing press, paper distribution of printed documents has given rise to all manner of problems.

The unpredictable nature of the market for a given document leads to great difficulties in predicting likely requirements for a first print run. This can lead to under-supply, or wasteful oversupply of a commodity that must be sold or borrowed to have any value.

In the world of business, the success of the photocopier and fax machine has taken care of much of the problem of instant printing, but this in itself leads to other problems, for example the cost of the copies, the lack of control in their production, the filing of multiple copies, the risk of using an out-of-date version, the potential for document leaks, the problem of 'wait states' which are implicit in the use of paper documents in a decision process where the paper itself lies dormant in an in-basket or in the post for a large percentage of its useful life.

Reliance on paper can also be extremely risky in the occasionally violent world in which we live. In two massive bomb incidents in the City of London near Bishopsgate vital business documents were to be seen among the ensuing rubble scattered over many acres and were irretrievably lost. Several businesses stopped trading because they could not recover the documents which were their only trading records.

With book sales and photocopiers both selling well we are still a long way from replacing print as the major information distribution medium. But we are witnessing strong interest in electronic document production, and the concept of instant publishing and printing-on-demand is beginning to re-define the marketplace.

Electronic viewing

One of the main reasons why print will persist is the current limitations of electronic viewing technology.

Consider the problem of VDUs (visual display units) attached to most computers. The first thing that strikes us is that they are wider than they are long. To look at a typical document, it would make sense to turn the VDU on its side which would give you a viewing window into which might just about fit an A4 page of text.

Most VDUs are too small for handling documents adequately. When you create a viewing window in an application, to view the pages of a document, you need to scroll the text of any page at least once to see the bottom half. While some early word processing systems recognized the need for full text page displays, the idea has not gained credence in the hardware market. The only comfortable answer is a large high-resolution colour monitor, but they are so large that they take up the whole desk and they will be much more expensive than the rest of your workstation.

However much you pay for high-resolution monitors, you are still faced with the problem of clarity when viewing on screen as opposed to printed text. The normal VDU technology supplied with the personal computer on the desktop is fine for the most part, but not recommended for constant or even high levels of reading. Producing documents which are designed to be used electronically is not simply a question of transfer of paper printing on to the VDU screen. One is a question of limited display lines as we have already mentioned. There is the issue of choice of typeface and layout with the recommendation that we use only certain fonts and font mixes to aid the process of reading on screen. A detailed review of these techniques is to be found in a Datapro report on the subject.[11]

The use of colour, available only to a small subset of printed documents, can greatly enhance the visual and cultural acceptability of electronic documents. If colour monitors become the norm, perhaps this may compensate users for the lack of an appropriate screen size and shape and for the problem of resolution levels.

Finally, we may have to give up some concepts concerning documents which have held sway since the first books were printed. The concept of a page may no longer be relevant at all. The most successful electronic books have dropped the idea of the page metaphor completely. The electronic 'page' is a virtual page, which is determined by (a) the number of lines your VDU can display, and (b) the contents to be brought together as a screen view by the system. The idea of the compound document - which is effectively a set of separately held elements such as text, tables, graphics and diagrams – delivers a 'page' or electronic view only at the point when we decide we need to display something.

Publishing and Printing On-Demand

Many organizations committed to producing large-volume and high-value documentation are investing in on-demand printing, for example computer software companies, aircraft manufacturers, automotive manufacturing companies and a whole host of defence-related producers. Here, the photocopier becomes a high-speed intelligent printing press. The software driving these machines is highly sophisticated and allows the integration of general purpose document management systems which control the various objects such as text and graphics in databases. The documents are created and managed using the document management software, and normally the users will access this information electronically either in client-server mode connecting a workstation or PC to a central or remote server, or using a standalone or shared CD-ROM. The information is quite often fully indexed by all the fixed attributes required for retrieval, and some documents will offer full-text search for additional value. The hypertext technique discussed earlier will also be used here to best effect to provide a non-linear means by which to move around the electronic books.

Demand printing will only take place when it is necessary to request a finite and known number of printed copies, for example to go out with the product such as a car manual or aircraft maintenance manual. From a workstation connected via the network to the print-on-demand system, a simple request to produce the required copies is generated. This simplicity of course hides the complex set of macro commands which will give rise to the document printing and collation process incorporating complex graphics, colour, indexing, contents page make-up, page layout and so on.

Uniting the players

There can be little doubt that the most important way to add value to the plethora of information media and sources, and to ensure its active use in organizations, is through professional information people. The technology by itself is simply the means, and they are the ones who know how best to use it. However, the professionals involved in all kinds of document and information work are scattered over a range of identifiable disciplines, each having its own somewhat restrictive views on what constitutes their brand of the information profession in question.

Librarians have long been urged to 'reject collecting as an end in itself' as Donald Urquart put it in his *Principles of Librarianship*[12], and few would subscribe to the view that 'the end of libraries could be to accept a museological role and see out the printed era', a choice whimsically suggested for them by James Thompson in his book *The End of Libraries* in 1992[13]. However, it may be interesting to speculate to what extent the professionals, the publishers and others traditionally involved in the information scene have been missing the opportunity.

Fortunately, many of those currently engaged in information activity tend to reject the traditional labels and the stereotypes. But despite the best efforts of librarians, archivists and others who may individually strive to broaden the role and break the moulds the professions have used on them, there is a tendency for us as users to reinforce the old order, for example most of us still feel humble in the presence of such collected wisdom and we have never really been very sure about why these people are special.

Management in all organizations needs to be courageous in challenging the professions, and their traditional views of their role, to find a better fit with the information needs emerging in managing the fourth resource. They might start that process by looking at, for example, where they locate their information centres, libraries records departments and so on. If they are generally out of the mainstream, then it may be time to re-examine what is going on, with the aim of getting the information more directly into the hands and minds of those who need it most. After all, information without distribution is like a cart without a horse.

CONCLUSION

There can be no conclusion to the process of IT innovation since there is no singular beginning and no singular end. However, a review like this one would not be in character if we failed to pass at least a few comments on where we seem to be going. To argue on the one hand for value judgements in our document collections and fail to provide a few here might be seen as churlish.

Capture

It seems likely that the combination of imaging and OCR/ICR will continue to grow in stature as the market matures. Improvements in document creation software such as word processing and desktop publishing will incorporate new standards to enable the handling of graphics and complex format; in some industries, the stabilization of format through use of facilities such as SGML (standard generalized markup language) will underpin the movement towards the management of complex electronic documents. The gradual introduction of voice recognition and the ability to dictate to computers will change the nature of the market yet again. Senior executives will be more likely to accept technology of that type on their desks since it will not have the uncomfortable connection with keyboarding – still regarded as menial, secretarial work. It seems that deeply ingrained cultural values continue to outlive attempts to redefine occupational roles.

Distribution

There can be little doubt that electronic documents are here to stay. A key feature will be the degree to which they achieve acceptance in the education field. Until now, teachers and educators have suffered badly from earlier attempts to introduce IT into the schools. Many teachers seem disenchanted with both the technology and the way they were introduced to it and most of the children are still caught up in the use of computers for home entertainment. The fascination for younger children (and some adults) with the computer game still dominates the scene but we are now seeing a growing interest in educational software, CD-ROM titles, on-line search and retrieval, and project-based learning. With the large investments in this area from publishers and from companies such as Microsoft, we should be able to look forward to a far greater opportunity for electronic information distribution.

The growth of on-line networking such as Internet opens up a whole new way of communication between individuals and companies. This type of communication escapes most of the restrictions imposed on printing and broadcasting and crosses international boundaries at will. It has led to concern, for instance the recent use of computer networks by neo-Nazi groups in Germany and elsewhere has led to interest in how the intelligence services can monitor what illegal information activity is going on in these networks. Most people would argue that the benefits of such an open and democratic communication channel should outweigh the occasional threat it provides from unscrupulous groups and individuals, but we expect that governments will soon be deciding what you can and can't do with your computer!

In industry, particularly where there is a need for technical documentation to be produced as a fundamental part of the production and quality control process, electronic distribution of documents is a fast-growing market. It represents cost reduction, competitive edge and business process refinement.

Despite the shortcomings described earlier of the viewing hardware, economics will force more and more of us to rely on electronic viewing. Quite simply, the luxury of paper will entail extra cost and extra effort.

Storage

Advances in digital storage techniques continue to produce magnetic and optical solutions that provide more and more capacity for less invested dollars. The key in terms of document management is the availability of cheap mass storage options which should herald the end of microfilm and older storage methods. What will finally give this market the boost it is waiting for is the acceptability of a document image as legal evidence. One would expect this now to be settled in the next few years, with a British Standard already drafted and an ISO standard following closely[14] Acceptance of these by the courts could have the effect of opening the floodgates.[15]

Retrieval

While various suppliers and specialists argue about which technique is preferable the market will quickly accept any level of text retrieval as long as it is attractive and easy to use, provides the basic means to locate the content of documents and a means of presenting the findings in some order of relevance. The majority of documents produced on CD-ROM will carry full text retrieval capability, and acceptance of the idea by electronic publishers means that the technology will be more or less commoditized. There still will be a considerable market for the specialist text retrieval products which offer particular strengths in given situations, for instance the ability to deal with very large volumes, the combination of structured and full-text searching, the need for highly structured thesauri and similar search controls.

Above all, ability to add value to document collections of all kinds will be seen as the major breakthrough. The combination of multimedia (the bringing together of text, graphics and sound) together with the facilities for full-text retrieval and hypertext is a powerful recipe for a redefinition of the learning process.

And finally

Information technology has led to very considerable gains in productivity in the blue-collar area of production and manufacturing.[16] On the white-collar side, despite a high quantity of investment in group and personal computing in nearly every office, productivity has been raised by a staggeringly low 4 per cent. But as we move progressively into general acceptance of the need for electronic document management across most sectors, we can look for dramatic changes in that figure. There are still far too many people involved in the 'paper-chase' that is the office and administration side of business. As organizations in all sectors embrace the technology now available to solve the problem, the world of business and commerce will be turned inside out in the quest for effective management of the fourth resource. In that process it will be necessary to challenge all the established information professions, abolishing the tendency to stereotype, and confront them until they are fully involved in transferring their essential skills and services.

It would be quite wrong to assume that this will be a bloodless revolution. Many companies will go out of business as they fail to understand that many of their clerical staff are no longer necessary. The public services will suffer even more. The Police Force, for example, is still using typewriters and has a mass of other incomprehensible investment in interim IT solutions. The health sector, typical of many public services, is weighed down by the thousands of tons of paper medical records it generates every year.

The message to management and educators everywhere is clear and urgent. There is a formidable challenge to us all in coming to terms with the information revolution in our schools, universities and all types of organizations. As the new generation of young people move into management, unafraid of technology and more aware of how to exploit it commercially, we should witness a redefinition of learning, innovation, and the nature of work. Those in charge of managing the fourth resource today have to face this challenge. Fundamentally, they have to be brave enough to believe that they can become the architects of tomorrow's workplace, and they will have to move fast.

NOTES

1   R Silverstone, 'Domesticating the Revolution: Information and Everyday Life', *Aslib Proceedings*, **45** (9), September 1993, pp. 227-33. D Ronfeldt. 'Cyberocracy is Coming', *Information Society*, **8** (4), October/December 1992, pp. 243–96. W.B. Raymond (ed.), 'The Legacy of Paul Otlet: Pioneer of Information Science,' an edited collection of Paul Otlet's essays in *Australian Library Journal*, **41** (2), May 1992, pp. 90–102.

2   J. Popkin and A. Cushman, 'Integrated Document Management Controlling a Rising Tide', *Gartner Group OIS Strategic Analysis Report R-IDM-117*, 3 September 1993.

3   K. Marx, *Das Capital*.

4   T.M. Koulopoulos and C. Frappaolo, *Imaging – the Risks and Benefits: A Survival Guide*, Delphi Consulting Group, 1992. (Based on a survey of 300 users in Fortune 1000 companies.)

5   *Electronic Documents*, **2** (9), September 1993 is a special issue dedicated to covering OCR and ICR and related matters.

6   J.H. Ashford and P. Willets, *Text Retrieval and Document Databases*, Bromley: Chartwell-Bratt, 1988.

7   R. Evans, 'Beyond Boolean: Relevance Ranking, Natural Language and the New Search Paradigm'. Proceedings of the 15th National Online Meeting, New York, 10-12 May1994, pp. 121–8.

8   T.H. Nelson, *Literary Machines, the Report on, and of, Project Xanadu*, Swarthmore, 1984.

9   V. Bush, 'As we may think', *Atlantic Monthly*, **176** (1), 1942, 101–8.

10 N. MacMorrow and P. Baird, 'Hypertext and Hypermedia', *Information Management*, **3** (1), 1993, 46–66.

11 *Datapro. Publication design for effective communication*, Workgroup Computing Series: Information Delivery, March 1994.
12 D. Urquhart, *Principles of Librarianship*, Bardsay, Leeds: Garth, 1981.
13 J. Thompson, *The End of Libraries*, London: C. Bingley, 1992.
14 G. Tapper, 'Legal Admissability of WORM based Electronic Document Images', *Document Management Europe*, **6** (6), June 1993, 1–2.
15 R. Dixon, 'Legal Admissability and Probative Value of Document Images', *Information Management and Technology*, **27** (1), January 1994, pp. 38–40.
16 Gartner Group use these figures in various studies.
17 Gartner reference 4% productivity.

Part III

INFORMATION MANAGEMENT IN THE REAL WORLD

The next three chapters deal with the practicalities of information management in the real world. In the first, Bill Cook, Partner with Ernst and Young in London, describes his experience with the development of an IM initiative in the Cabinet Office of the UK government.

In the second chapter Dr Brian Collins discusses the practical issues of defining and managing systems for information in the context of a range of management imperatives. As Director of Strategic Information Systems for the Wellcome Foundation and a former Partner in the consulting firm of KPMG he has wide experience of the subject as both consultant and practitioner.

Peter Vickers is one of the most experienced information management specialists in the country today, and it is fitting that in the final paper in this part of the book it should be Peter who highlights the problems and pitfalls which all too often bedevil our attempts to manage information effectively.

6 Selling information management as value for money

Bill Cook

HOW IT ALL BEGAN

It was in 1984 (an interesting but not directly relevant date) when I was first asked the question, 'What does information management mean to you?' I had just been appointed to head a branch in the Cabinet Office's Management and Efficiency Division and the person who posed the question was my new boss. Not unnaturally I was keen to make a good impression and I therefore struggled to come up with a credible and worthwhile reply. I failed. For the life of me I could not construct a response which brought together my knowledge of information – primarily at that time concerned either with computers (remember the 'multi-function workstation' was at that time the great innovation!) or with producing meaningful and 'sound' ministerial briefs (I had spent some time in a policy division of the DTI) and management (having been in on the ground floor of the Financial Management Initiative (FMI), I had learnt the mantra of the three Es – economy, efficiency and effectiveness – but no one had defined them yet!).

WHY NOT THE 'NORMAL' CENTRAL APPROACH TO INITIATIVES?

Despite this, and somewhat improbably, I was confirmed in my post – which suggested to me that no one else had much of an idea of information management either. My task (and I was not given the choice of whether or not to accept it) was to develop policy for information management and ensure that it was taken up across government. This would of course be easy, all I had to do was to write a well-constructed paper littered with references to texts and explain to government departments that they were to implement information management across their operations and report back on progress in six months.

As I have mentioned, however, I was heavily involved in the early days of the FMI and as such had been on the receiving end of many helpful notes on that subject. I had, as I imagine had others, worried about how to develop and promulgate a policy for a while before it occurred to me that any broadly sensible reply would do.

Why was this? To understand the answer it is important to understand the way in which central initiatives were launched in those far-off days (having been out of the Civil Service for more than seven years now I am not qualified to comment on whether or not this remains the case). Basically, someone would come up with a good idea ('We're not terribly good at managing finance in government, wouldn't it be splendid if we were a lot better at it – I'll bet the private sector have something to offer'). Next someone would give it a name (FMI, Human Resource Development, Information Management) and persuade someone important that it was worth doing; they would then be made the 'supremo' of the initiative and be given a team of people whose own careers would then turn on the success of the the initiative. Next, departments would be told to get on with it and be told that the 'centre' would be monitoring their progress. Very sensibly, the departments would appoint someone from the private sector to advise and support them. The external appointees would then do their best to make something happen. Eventually, the predefined milestones would appear and reports would be required. However:

- Departments were going to have to report to the centre, so they would hardly have wished to challenge any statements that 'good progress had been made' – they too had no interest in reporting 'little change'.
- The initiative team, whose careers depended on the the success of the initiative, were also disinclined to make waves – the departments they were responsible for had made 'good progress'.
- The 'supremo' heard that good progress was being made in all quarters – just what he or she had expected when the idea first occured – positive change on all fronts. It was time for an enthusiastic report to the Minister.

So why not do the same thing with information management? I felt strongly that this would not be the way to progress in this instance for two reasons. First, I had not thought the idea up – merely inherited it – so I had no personal interest in a success at that stage and was keen to see if real change could be made to happen. Second, my posting was for three years and I was unconvinced that I could keep up a steady flow of 'good progess' reports for three years without anyone noticing that not much had happened. Well, for whatever reason, I concluded that I would have a go at really making some changes. How this was done (and I think some real changes were made) is the subject of this chapter.

My task then was to 'sell' information management to the Civil Service which was already suffering from 'initiative overload', which fundamentally mistrusted anything coming out of the 'centre' and which, in general, had very little idea of what was meant by information management in the first place.

What is information management?

As I saw it, my first task was to get a grip on what I meant by information management – on the well-established marketing principle (I will return to marketing principles later) that a good salesman must first sell his product to himself. I read much and met a lot of people, ranging from academics to computer companies. The responses I obtained were of some help, but quite limited help, at that time.

There was an interesting academic argument going on at the time which focused on the difference between data and information. Data, I came to understand, were (note the plural) raw facts which only became 'information' when they were used. I struggled for a while to differentiate between data management and information management - the former concerned with efficiency and economy (clearly there would be no effectiveness element involved in managing something which by definition was not used) and the latter with effectiveness. I concluded that this did not work very well since it was clearly not effective to have collected and stored your data so efficiently that it was not available for use; equally information could be uneconomic if it was unnecessary to the decision made (the third time you use information to prove what you already know is not very economic use of the resource either) and inefficient if it was used to persuade the wrong person of the validity of a position.

The computer companies were at that time very keen on the concept of the 'information centre' as the route to information management. In effect, the role of the information manager was to ensure that 'users' could access all the information resources of the organization through a single computer screen. This seemed to me to be a good thing but perhaps a touch Utopian (I had also been involved in the DTI 'Office of the Future' pilot projects and none of these – to my certain knowledge - had created anything even approaching the paperless office ideal). This approach seemed to ignore information which had never and would never be computerized. One of our largest corporations had estimated that more than half of their information resources would remain in paper form well into the next century – clearly a management discipline which took no account of the majority of the resource it sought to manage would not offer the whole answer.

However, two key pieces of information did emerge from all these discussions. The first of these was my idea. I thought of a phrase which summed up my understanding of what information management was about: 'Information management is concerned with obtaining the best possible value for money from an organization's information resources.'

'Value for money' (VFM) had a nice ring to it (and was already recognized as a 'good thing' across the Civil Service). It meant that I could apply VFM thinking to all aspects of information and expect to come up with answers which, depending on the aspect of information it addressed, improved economy, *103* efficiency and effectiveness. 'Information resources' seemed to me to cover both data and information and to include all information irrespective of the media on which it was recorded.

The second key input which emerged from my process of investigation was the concept of the information or record life cycle. I am not certain where this idea first came from but I heard it first from Xerox and am happy to acknowledge this (with apologies to anyone else who thought of it first). Basically this concept suggests that all information, or records, pass through five stages:

1 *Creation*. In this stage information is created (by original thought, survey, investigation, or the consolidation of existing information or data). It costs money, time and effort to create information but, at the point of creation it adds no value.

2 *Communication*. In this stage, the created information or record is transmitted to others (by word of mouth, letter, memo, telephone, fax, e-mail, etc.). Again there are costs involved but at this stage, if through no other means than by adding to the sum of human knowledge, a certain amount of value is added.

3 *Use*. In this stage the information is used (to make decisions, to persuade others, to report on performance, etc.). There are costs associated with this stage but this is the time at which information value is at its greatest.

4 *Storage*. After use, information is stored (in records centres, registries, computers, microfilm libraries, etc.). Cost is again very significant here – especially in the Civil Service environment in which information can be retained for up to 25 years (and even then it may be transferred to the Public Records Office and held even longer); but, referring back to stage one, the information can have value if it is retrieved to be, form part of, or contribute to the creation of new information.

5 *Disposal*. At a given point – where the possiblity of retrieval for the creation of new information has reduced to a very low level - information is disposed of. Clearly there is no value at this stage but there is cost. Where the information is in any way sensitive the process of disposal itself may be expensive. In any case, someone has to decide that information can be disposed of and the time involved in that decision-making process carries costs. Also, at this stage, is risk. Risk of disposing of information whose capacity for value (to the current organization or future generations) has not been exhausted.

It seemed to me that this combination of the concept of value for money in the management of information resources with the five-stage life cycle offered a way forward in making information management an idea which I could sell to myself and therefore to others.

Creation

VFM in the creation of information meant focusing on the costs of the process. How could you reduce that cost? Well, clearly I could not do a lot to influence the quality of original thought, although some of the more recent thinking surrounding business process innovation and re-engineering suggests that there are ways to do this); my focus, however, was on the ways in which information might be re-used rather than re-invented. It seemed obvious to me that an organization that knew what information it had already created and re-used was likely to be significantly more efficient in the creation of information than one which did not.

Additionally, it was going to be essential that information about the same thing was called by the same name – otherwise how would the information creator know whether he or she needed to use existing information. This drew me into naming conventions (already well established in the context of computer data management) and the use of consistent indexing systems for paper and microfilm records.

Overall this meant that efficiency in information creation could be enhanced by the use of tools and techniques surrounding information on information (which I subsequently discovered was called 'meta-information').

Communication

VFM in the communication of information meant two things:

1   Knowing who needed to know the information you had created and ensuring that it reached all of those people (so maximizing the value of the communications process) and that it did not waste the time of people who did not need to know it (so minimizing the uneconomic aspects of communications). This meant that an idea such as a task-oriented rather than alphabetic directory was going to be a very important information management tool.
2   Using the most efficient means of communicating information and reducing to the minimum these costs. This meant that the technology of communication was very much part of information management – including not just the high-tech end either, but also telephones, messenger services, inter- and intra-departmental post services.

Use

VFM in the use of information had, primarily, to be about ways of increasing the value of the information. Presentational tools were clearly important, since these were concerned with ensuring that the message contained in the information was received by the listener quickly and effectively.

Storage

Possibly the trickiest area since there needed to be an equal focus on efficient storage and effective retrieval. The media was significant too – efficient storage and effective retrieval worked well on computers (so long as you had bought enough memory) but tests had proved that finding where things were on computers was less straightforward than might have been expected. Equally, transferring information from paper to computer might save space but was – at that time at least – an expensive process. Lastly, from the perspective of public records, the 'over-write' capability of computers, while leaving us with a neat and tidy product, would lose the observations and marginal comments of officials and Ministers so beloved of historians.

Similar factors applied to microfilm (with the added joy that microfilm tends to distort after a period if not kept in correct environmental condition, so long-term storage on this medium might carry with it the additional cost of re-filming after some time).

Paper was even more difficult – this was a physical medium (which had very considerable advantages in legal matters) and would be of little value unless it could be placed in front of a user (as opposed to magnetic and microfilm media which could be accessed from a distance). However, the storage of paper in the prime office space was very expensive and its storage in distant records stores very cheap. A fine balance would need to be struck here and a set of techniques concerned with identifying the likelihood of retrieval would clearly be an advantage.

The ways in which paper was stored would have an impact on costs. For example a hanging filing cabinet could store five times as much paper on the same floor space as two drawer filing cabinets. Again advice on efficient storage was going to be an important element of information management.

Overall, within the storage stage, there were issues concerning the selection of the appropriate media, methods of identifying and retrieving stored information, ways of establishing the level of need for information retrieval and the relative costs of information storage.

Disposal

The VFM issue here was concerned with when to dispose. So long as the decision was put off the costs of storage would continue; equally if the decision were taken too early there would be risks associated with subsequent creation costs. I was particularly interested in this, given a short period on the UK negotiating team seeking to persuade the French that they were responsible for a rather larger element of the costs of the Concorde project than they cared to admit. In that instance I needed to access Concorde files going back to 1959 – if these had been disposed of we would have been forced to rely purely on French records which might not have improved our negotiating position! There was little doubt that tools and techniques associated with the definition of disposal of information would make a substantial contribution to efficiency in this area. Interestingly, the paper records' managers were considerably in advance of their IT colleagues in this area and there was a strong foundation for building such tools in the methods and techniques readily available in the 'Cinderella' area of records and registry management.

At this point I had what I believed would be a coherent argument that the information life cycle carried with it at its various stages both costs and value; that in every case value for money could be improved through enhancing the value where appropriate and reducing the costs; and that there were tools and techniques available (or developable) which could deliver those improvements.

I felt, therefore, that I was in a position to say to departments, 'Manage your information better' and to answer the two ripostes: 'What do you mean by "manage your information"?' and 'How do we do it "better"?'

An information managment marketing strategy

My next issue was therefore to work out how to sell this message to the Civil Service. I had long been convinced that central dictats seldom win hearts and minds and I was particularly convinced that in the case of information management I had to persuade people that I was offering them something that would genuinely improve the performance of their organisation. I therefore turned to marketing principles again.

I want to mention three main principles of marketing:

1　There needs to be competition for marketing techniques to be applicable. (I ask you to compare the level of advertising in the telecommunications industry – lots of competition – with that in the water industry – local monopolies – to confirm the significance of competition to the level of marketing required.) Did competition exist in the area of information management? With what or with whom was I competing? I struggled with this for a while. After all I did not regard the efforts of my IT colleagues to encourage better data management or those in records management to develop good disposal schedules as competition – rather I saw them as complementary efforts. I finally recognized my competition, and it is, I believe, the same competition as is faced by anyone seeking to deliver change initiatives in a large organization – inertia. Inertia is very strong in any large organization and it does, quite explicitly, compete with change and seek to prevent it or to minimize it. I therefore identified inertia as my competitor and set about beating it in the marketplace.

2　All markets can and should be segmented into groups of people who will, broadly, respond to the same stimuli in the same way. Having looked at my marketplace, the Civil Service, I identified that different groups of people would respond to information management in different ways:

- Policy-oriented staff, who would respond by asking how informaton management could help them do their work better. This segment would be attracted by effectiveness arguments.
- Line managers, who were just receiving the responsibilities and authority associated with delegated budgets and who would respond by asking how information management could help them get more for less. This segment would be attracted by efficiency arguments.
- Resource managers, particularly those responsible for personnel and estates management, who would respond by asking how information management could help them save money, people or space. This segment would be attracted by economy arguments.

3　The third principle of marketing is that within each of the above segments we can distinguish four groups of influencers:

(a)   The *innovators*, people (probably about 5–10 per cent of the population) who were attracted to new ideas by their newness, not by any considered evaluation of the quality of the ideas. These people could be expected to support information management but their enthusiasm would last only as long as it took for a new 'new idea' to come along. At the same time the support of these people would be likely to put off everyone else in the organization who would assume that information management was just the next in a long line of enthusiasms which would wear off soon.

(b)   The *opinion leaders*, people (probably about 10–25 per cent of the population) who would consider new ideas and after due thought put their weight behind those which they felt would be of value to the organization. They could be expected to support information management if its value were demonstrated and their support would be both sustained over the longer term and acknowledged by the organization as a signal that the initiative was worth pursuing.

(c)   The *majority*, people (probably about 50–60 per cent of the population) who could be expected to follow the opinion leaders over time.

(d)   The *laggards*, people (probably about 20–25 per cent of the population) who would not be budged from inertia on information management. Time spent with these people was almost certainly going to be time wasted. However, the rest of the organization would recognize the status of these people and would not be put off by their lukewarm response. Eventually, when information management became part of the accepted way of doing things, they would adopt it.

With this thinking behind me I set about developing an information management marketing strategy which focused on identifying the opinion leaders in each of my three segments and demonstrating to them that information management was an important element of resource management within their organizations.

There were two further aspects of the strategy which are worth mentioning.

First, and critically, it was essential, notwithstanding the specific element of information management I was pursuing within the segment, to explain that this was part of an overall information management activity which contained all three of the elements of value for money – economy, effectiveness and efficiency. I was interested in selling the whole change through one of its components, not just the component itself; I therefore created a short explanatory paper which placed each of the components in the overall information management context. When addressing a particular segment I covered the paper with a note bringing out the particular advantages of information management likely to appeal to the segment in question.

Second, it was important to recognize that the innovator–opinion leader–majority–laggard split applied to the Civil Service as a whole as well as to the people within departments. So certain departments were regarded as innovators, others laggards and others opinion leaders. This categorization may well have changed since I carried out the research which underpinned my marketing strategy so I will not say which department fell into which category at the time. I will, however, assert that this subdivision of departments (and agencies within departments) still exists and that it is important to find out in any organization which department or individual is where within these categories.

How did I carry out the research?

It was remarkably straightforward in practice. I used contacts in most government departments to ask the following question with a view to determining the opinion leader departments:

> Assume that you have prepared a brief for your senior manager which suggests that a particular initiative or idea is a good one; the senior manager attends an inter-departmental meeting on the subject; which two or three departments representatives speaking before your senior manager against the idea would cause him or her to modify their brief significantly (that is, to say he or she was neutral on the issue when you had recommended in favour)?

I checked this question out with a dozen or so departmental contacts and identified a remarkably consistent set of 'opinion leading departments' on whom my marketing strategy was to concentrate.

Delivering the strategy: demonstration projects

With my strategy established I set about its implementation. I needed to demonstrate to opinion leaders in each of my segments that information management would deliver what they wanted or needed. I set about achieving this through three carefully planned projects which were set up on the following basis:

- Each project had to have a clear objective focused on the delivery of VFM in information management using replicable tools and techniques which addressed the key concerns of the opinion leaders within the relevant segment.
- Each project had to have measurable success criteria which could be subject to subsequent review.
- Each project had to have a high profile within the organization. Since I was confident of success I wanted a high profile; if I had not been confident of success I would not have 'sold' the idea to myself and should not have been doing the thing in the first place! In my view far too many such demonstration projects are taken forward in areas of low risk and low profile; when they work well no one knows about it and no one cares (thus undermining the whole point of the demonstration in the first place), when they do not work, no one knows about it either and further experiments and demonstrations go ahead (instead of simply stopping work on things which aren't delivering).

So what were the projects and how did they work out?

EFFECTIVENESS

The effectiveness project was directed at the top management of an opinion-leading department (very high profile!). Its intention was to deliver the information on the performance of the department and the external economic and environmental factors which impacted upon departmental performance. Its prime criteria was that this information should be delivered without the need to collect any information which was not already available to the department.

The project began by establishing what information the top managers needed. Here was the first problem. Classic information needs analysis and data modelling techniques did not work particularly well. Interestingly a data model of top managers' information needs ends up looking very like the data model for the department as a whole. This is not only hugely complex and very difficult to verify with the top managers but also misses the point that top managers want to know a little about a lot and the tricky bit is the definition of the little not the documentation of the lot.

We took the project forward by presenting to the top managers our assessment of what they needed on a set of paper charts populated with entirely invented data (it would clearly not have represented good value for money to invest time and effort in drawing together a wide range of real information only to find that the top managers did not want it!). The top managers (like top managers across the Civil Service) were much more comfortable commenting on a draft than responding to a blank sheet of paper and were able to modify our first charts in a way which reflected their needs. Having established the desired outputs we set about locating and drawing together just the information needed to deliver those outputs. Within a very few weeks we were able to deliver the outputs required, this time populated with real data.

Ninety per cent of the information required was available in-house; the remaining 10 per cent would need to be collected but only that 10 per cent was required. We had minimized collection costs and delivered a product which maximized value for money by using information management techniques surrounding information creation.

The next stage was to look at the presentation of the information (maximizing value from use). We investigated various options (and indeed retained paper as a delivery mechanism until suitable technological alternatives emerged) and ultimately transferred the product to a 'packaged' executive information system. This system, suitably modified and changed in the light of changing circumstances, is still in use almost a decade later in the department and is regarded as an essential management tool.

EFFICIENCY

The efficiency demonstration concerned a department with a wide variety of information held on a wide variety of different computer- and paper-based systems. Among other things the department was concerned with the identification of organizations who were at risk of failing to meet their statutory responsibilites. Such organizations were visited and the department sought to focus each visit effectively. Our project sought to provide more for less by using better communications, naming and retrieval techniques to deliver greater efficiency in the focusing and use of visiting officers' time.

Again, we undertook this in a way which maximized value for money in itself. Rather than developing and implementing complex computer and telecommunications systems and installing complex data management and records indexing policies before demonstrating their value, we set up a small group to bring together all of the information which might be useful to visiting officers or visit selection. We physically constructed the packages of information required for these purposes for a limited and controlled experimental period.

The experimental period delivered a range of results which demonstrated precisely where IT and data management policies would add value to the process; and just as importantly where they would not. Subsequent developments within the department have followed the routes suggested by the experiment and are now delivering improved value for money in the creation, communication and retrieval of information.

ECONOMY

The economy experiment focused on a department in the process of rationalizing its estate. There was a clear need and a clearly measurable requirement to ensure that as little space as possible was wasted in the new buildings the department expected to move to. We associated ourselves with the estates planning process and implemented the full range of storage and disposal VFM techniques.

We helped the department decide:

- what information it could afford to dispose of (and to establish disposal schedules over the longer term for all of its information);
- what was the most appropriate storage medium for the information it wished to retain, taking into account the space costs of paper and, to a lesser extent, microfilm, the memory costs associated with computer storage and the conversion costs associated with moving from paper to either computers or microfilm;
- if paper was the selected medium, where the records could be stored (close to users for immediate retrieval, further away when retrieval could take longer);
- if paper storage close to users was selected, which storage devices would deliver the best volume of storage/space ratio.

The effect of our involvement was both that entire new floors of space were created. Further departments followed this lead and were able to report millions of pounds of savings year on year as a result of applying these value for money techniques in the storage and disposal of information.

And then what happened?

These and a number of other carefully planned, well-publicized and successful experiments created a group of opinion leaders in the Civil Service who were   *111* convinced of the need for information management. By the end of my time in the Cabinet Office the information management initiative had been established and, as I have worked with departments on a range of assignments since my own move to consultancy, I am struck by how many of the concepts and VFM techniques we helped identify (I do mean identify, I claim original thinking for my team on very few of the techniques and tools currently operating in government) are now in full operation and are accepted (even by the laggards) as the way things are done.

A few examples are worthy of reference. Records management (as opposed to registry supervision) is now a clear government discipline – with records managers across government demonstrating through the current round of market tests that they are able to deliver a service which is more attuned to the needs of their departments and is more efficient than that on offer from the private sector. The Civil Service is, I believe, now firmly among the leaders in the delivery of value for money in the management of information resources held on paper.

Executive information systems, based on the exploitation of existing information resources rather than off-line information collection, are becoming more and more a feature of senior managers' offices. These have achieved a record of continuing use and success which is significantly greater than their equivalents in the private sector. Again the Civil Service has established a strong position in the delivery of value for money in the creation and presentation for use of information.

Across government, the key elements of data management and naming conventions have developed significantly. Increasingly, the data dictionaries created and maintained in departments and agencies are moving away from their 'pure' IT roots and are playing their parts in the development of cross-departmental and cross-agency working. At the same time data dictionaries are becoming smaller, better focused on those items of information in which the expense of maintaining control is justified by the value of doing so to both systems developers and the government as a whole. Value for money is increasingly being delivered in the areas of creation, communication and retrieval as a result.

But what of information management itself? Notwithstanding the developments in respect of the components of information management, I believe that information management is still to emerge fully as a clearly understood discipline in its own right. There is little doubt that it has entered the lexicon of government and is seen as an important aspect of resource management. Additionally, many businesses in the public sector and beyond are now focusing on information management as a source of competitive advantage. On the other hand the marketing task remains – to demonstrate that the thinking processes which created the developments discussed above are part of the single information management discipline; that successes in delivering value for money in one area of the management of the information resource can be effectively translated into other areas by the application of value for money thinking to the various stages of the information life cycle.

So did it work?

It is worth comparing the impact of marketing information management with that of the progress of the FMI (which, it will be recalled began significantly earlier). The FMI has had White Papers, numerous reports, and a tremendous level of central drive. Despite this, departments remain concerned that their staff do not take financial management as seriously as they should, and financial delegation remains at a low level in many departments; critically, the savings which in-house teams have been able to identify when faced with competition through market testing suggest that the FMI missed opportunities for 25 per cent savings and more. I am driven to the conclusion that the method of marketing the FMI at the time delivered a very high profile and a good deal of lip-service.

The method of marketing information management, on the other hand, has not delivered profile, but it does seem to have generated change with very considerably less cost and effort. I am clearly biased here, but while I would certainly have preferred a higher profile for the discipline (and remain hope-ful that this will come), I feel that the approach to selling the ideas underlying information management has been successful in practice if not in publicity!

Eight steps to marketing information management

It may be useful to summarize the steps I went through in developing and implementing the information management marketing strategy:

1   Ensure that you understand what it is you are trying to sell. (I feel happy with applying VFM thinking to the five stages of the information life cycle but you may find other concepts easier to deliver.)
2   Work out how what you are trying to sell will work. (Identify, clarify and document the techniques involved so you can answer the question 'How do I do it then?')
3   Recognize that your competition is not some other initiative or some other division but that it is inertia in your own organization.
4   Segment your marketplace into the groups who will respond well to different marketing messages and work out (and test) what those messages are.
5   Establish who and what are the opinion-leading individuals and groups within your organization.
6   Set up high-profile demonstrations to prove the strength of your information management case which address the key requirements of the key opinion leaders.
7   Ensure that the demonstrations are seen as a demonstration of information management as a whole – not just the specific component.
8   Make sure you stay with the process after the opinion leaders are convinced.

Since I am now one of those external advisers who get called in when initiatives are launched I have a natural desire that the progress made on   *113* information management across government is maintained. But quite apart from that, I think that sufficient progress has now been made on many of the components of information management (with real successes to point to) and that information management has insinuated itself into the thinking of sufficient numbers of opinion leaders to make the time right for a series of marketing strategies to be launched across government and beyond. If you agree with me, I wish you luck and hope that the discussion above will provide some useful pointers – the process worked pretty well for me, it might do for you too!

7   Practicalities of information management

Dr Brian Collins

In this next, wide-ranging chapter, Brian Collins, formerly with KPMG Management Consultants, and now head of information systems at the Wellcome Trust, discusses the technological implications of the information revolution and hence the need for information management. He argues, much as did Bill Cook in the previous chapter, that if we are to derive value for money from our investments in the information-handling technologies, we have no choice but to manage information and to manage it properly.

After the initial discussion Dr Collins goes on to consider specific issues under the headings of information format and media, creation, ownership, storage and retrieval, manipulation, and communication, before drawing the chapter to a close with conclusions on integration.

Organizational change is occurring everywhere. The term *status quo* is not acceptable to almost all enterprises for a whole range of reasons, from political and regulatory through legal and technological to competitive and financial. The management of change, the empowerment of individuals and the re-engineering of business process are phrases that are extensively being used to describe the activities that represent this revolution in the way that groupings of 'scarce resources' in the classical economist's sense are being used. I refer to these as groupings because the concepts of firms, institutions, conglomerates, alliances and even nation states are being challenged by these changes. New words such as 'virtual corporations', 'workgroups' and 'enterprise villages' are being invented to describe these new structures. They all share a common feature; they share information, the new 'scarce resource' to enable them to deliver the benefits they perceive to be available via the structures they are part of.

In this chapter I shall discuss the factors and influences which have an impact on the changes now occurring in organizations in terms of the emergence of information management as a related set of concepts linking the key role of information in these re-engineered, flatter, organizations.

Information-based enterprises are the basis of these new groupings. The added value to all participants, financial, social, or political, comes from sharing information in a controlled and managed way rather than from the 'information is power' syndrome of keeping all information within a tightly constrained group. In this scenario there are significant penalties for not sharing information; there remain possibly fatal, in enterprise terms, penalties for allowing information to be 'given away' or 'lost'. Proactive information management is therefore a new and vital process alongside the other traditional business processes of financial control, manufacturing, logistics, buying and selling etc.

Flattened structures are a widely spoken of result of the revolutionary changes discussed above. This is another way of describing the fact that a process-driven view of a business results in a different way of laying out on a two dimensional diagram, how an organization actually works. It may look less hierarchical and hence flatter. The chains of 'command' in the military sense may be shorter. The re-engineering may have made the actual activities simpler, and the use of technology may have automated some of the tasks within the processes to the extent that they are no longer described except by the information systems department or the production engineering department. However, under all this apparent change, human nature will not have shifted very much at all. There will be individuals who like 'empires'. There will be those who like to be, and are, good leaders of groups of others. There are those who shudder at the thought of *not* being part of a group. The apparently new flattened structure may only be a different representation of the same processes connected together in a different way. The author's experience of reorganization in large public service organizations was that the changes in the organizational diagrams, that is, which division or group a unit was in, resulted in little change except poring over the new telephone directories to see where the people that 'we work with' had gone so that life could go on as before.

Those who are implementing changes that are *by design*, through the use of BPR and other new analytic approaches (Taylorism was one such approach), changing the nature of work, disregard the difficulties – some have to adopt new roles, responsibilities and ways of working – at their peril. This is not to say that a significant fraction of a workforce will not grasp the opportunities offered by such changes and deliver what is required.

But the new factor that will alter the nature of work is more fundamental and is, in part, connected to the concept that information shared, within a controlled set of processes, adds more value than information withheld. Withholding information is at one end of the spectrum of information management; crudely put, it is the 'I will not tell you this because you will use it against me'. It is an absolute embargo on dissemination. The other end of the spectrum is broadcasting of information; it is in the public domain and all can have it and use it for whatever purpose they need. 'Academic freedom' is an excellent example of a result of this approach. No judgement is used as to whether information should be managed. 'Broadcast and be damned' describes it all.

Controlled sharing of information demands a set of processes and approaches that have only started to be institutionalized in the last 20 years or so, mainly as a result of new technology, global communications, personal mobility and, maybe most importantly, an information explosion unprecedented in human history.

The speed of modern information systems (IS) has resulted in information being processed and displayed to users and manipulators of that information at unprecedented rates. Gone are the early days of computing when a batch run on the mainframe to get the month's financial results was run a week after the end of the month when the data had been entered on punched cards and, crashes permitting, was available on the financial director's desk ten days after month's end. Near real-time monitoring of cash flow of all branches of an organization is now technically feasible and is implemented for some 'just in time'(JIT) dependent organizations. The limit on the rate of use of information is limited only by the speed with which the human being can absorb the information presented, convert it to knowledge by combining it with other information previously memorized, and most importantly, to the subjective information derived from intuitive processes.

Reliable global communications have also resulted in the geographical distribution of the 'set of managed objects'[1] that make up the process being irrelevant. Inter-enterprise collaboration is greatly facilitated not only by telecommunications across the globe becoming available and more reliable, but also by high-speed air travel allowing people to personally interact and get to know each other well enough for sufficient trust to build up and allow mutually supportive but independent action to take place, even though the parties concerned are thousands of miles apart. This mobility and social mixing, combined with global telecommunications, has resulted in the phrase of 'global village'. A village is a social unit in which 'everybody knows everybody else's business'. The globe is a long way from this situation, but it would appear that a large number of global 'families' are being created as a result of these processes.

The explosion in the amount of information in the world comes from a number of sources but the two principle ones would appear to be the growth in world population and the increasing numbers in absolute terms, although not percentage terms, of literate and numerate people. Literacy and numeracy results in the ability to analyse and express original thought in forms that are communicable to others. Of course, artistic forms of expression that are not necessarily enabled by being literate and numerate are not to be excluded. Artistic creativity, expressed in image or sound, an indivisible part of civilized cultures and the information that such a process creates needs to be managed in the same way as alphanumeric-based information. The recent explosion in multimedia representations is the IS communities' response to this need. Capturing creative activities in forms that allow the product to be controlled and managed is a vital part of information management. Published books derive from original manuscripts, which in the early days of publishing were regarded, rightly, as priceless. Also valuable were the tools and processes of publishing, the printing press and the skills of typesetting. Controls and management of the modern methods of creation will be returned to later in this chapter.

Wealth creation comes from value being added to an assemblage of managed objects by the process of assemblage. A Rolls-Royce is perceived to be more valuable than its component parts because of the skills and experience that are put into the vehicle by the team who assemble it, if it can be sold at a price higher than the overall costs. Similarly, a movie is more valuable than the costs of the actors, the crew, props and special effects if the public in large enough numbers pay box office charges that exceed these costs. Assembling managed objects, that consist only of information, to make information assets that are more valuable than the sum of the parts is not yet seen as standard practice. The economics of information as the 'fourth' scarce resource are yet to be elucidated in forms that investors, accountants and lawyers can practice in their professions with confidence.

The management of information in this contextual setting is therefore affected by this uncertainty, and hence is difficult to justify in economic terms. Simple rules that apply to 'solid' managed objects seem to be inappropriate for information objects. Should simple scaling rules apply for part purchase? For example, is the telephone system for the whole of the UK more or less valuable than one for London? Does that value depend on the representation, electronic or paper, and whether or not it comes with an index or search tools? Should discounts apply for bulk purchase? If I buy 20 copies of the UK telephone directory, should I pay 20 times the creation cost, or only the material costs of replication? If in paper form there may be little difference, but on CD-ROM, or even more 'over a network', the economics of added value during replication are not clear at all. Every one of these features imply that despite the importance of information management, until they become clearly defined, investment in information management will continue to be less well justified than for other elements of business processes.

BUSINESS PROCESS

A principle reason for information management becoming a critical subject to modern business is a re-evaluation of Taylorism. This has shifted the emphasis of analytic activity from tasks to processes. This is combined with the realization that information is a critical contributor to the wealth creation process and, in spite of a well-developed formalism for economic description of wealth creation by use of information, benefits analysis and value chain analysis is carried out with information-based processes being critical elements. Drivers for this analysis are cost reduction, competitive advantage and optimization of process. These objectives all derive from the traditional approach of achieving internal optimization within the market sector that the organization operates.

In the last few years, as the ability to deal with changes in the marketplace, local and global politics and financial settings has become more important, flexibility in the way in which business processes are constructed has become a very important factor. In the context of information management, flexibility requirements result in a need for more flexible systems and more rapidly implemented software-based processes. The distributed environment, rapid prototyping of software and higher-level development languages are the IS industry's response.

Volume growth in world trade since the end of the Second World War has been enormous, partly due to population growth, partly to no major military conflicts between the western nations and partly to organizations such as GATT and OECD promoting the conditions for growth. Information growth has been a natural product of this activity, and with it new activities within the business process that use information as a critical element of the activity. Examples include market intelligence, market creation, competitor analysis, logistics support and customer profiling. Misuse or lose the information that supports these processes and an enterprise may find itself in difficulties, whether it be a commercial or government organization. Information management then becomes a critical process enabling strategic policy to be created. This policy itself then becomes part of the information asset of the organization. Handling knowledge about a business process as an asset is rapidly becoming a dominant information management activity, especially for information dominated enterprises such as software houses, broadcasting and media distribution.

The treatment of business as a system is a relatively old concept. What is relatively new is the ability to simulate and analyse the complexities of business processes, to take a methodical (as opposed to a methodological) approach to describing those parts of a business that can be so treated, recognizing that there will be parts that cannot (those that rely on judgement and intuition), and formulating a benefits-based approach to change that can be realized by a combination of revolution and evolution. This whole process itself is an example of information management, where the information is about processes, skills, objectives, external constraints and opportunities, and intrinsic and extrinsic information. The activity legitimizes the combination of systems analysis with the management of information and benefits analysis. It treats the business as a complete entity and takes full account of all the quantifiable and non-quantifiable constraints. Its success stems from technological reliability and scale, the perceived need for businesses to manage complexity and the availability of tools and methods for them to do so and, critically, the recognition that the fuel that enables all of this activity to happen is *information that is shared throughout the enterprise*.

Confidence in the success of this approach comes from the sharing process, resulting in extrinsic information being made more valuable. Phrases such as 'all singing from the same hymn sheet', 'I know a man who can', derive from shared information being perceived as critical to the success of the enterprise. Going beyond the internal 'range' of an organization to the external 'reach',[2] the management of information in a coherent way allows external confidence to be built up in an organization. This is vital for all stakeholders, be they shareholders in a public company, investors in a start-up, or followers of a political party.

THE IMPACT OF DIFFERING FORMATS AND MEDIA ON INFORMATION MANAGEMENT

The practicalities of managing information are affected by a large number of factors. The business world in the west is going through the transition from a paper-based society to a mixed, paper and electronic one. Different nations are at different stages of this transition, with the US probably in the lead. There is no doubt in most business people's minds that more and more information will be presented to them electronically, and even where the need to look at, say, 20 different documents to extract an overall set of information is still best done with paper, it will not be long before technology will allow the documents to be displayed in such a way as to emulate the paper-based approach.

Modern executives are much more mobile than their counterparts 20 years ago. It is now difficult to unravel whether they travel because that is where their business is or their business is where it is because they travel. The synergy between sectors, due in part to market intelligence and market generation discussed above, makes it difficult to unravel cause and effect. Nevertheless, additional factors in their ability to carry out their business wherever they are in the world are that, first, they can carry, view and manipulate a large amount of electronically stored information that is in a portable computer, much more than they ever could in the form of paper, and second, they can access missing information by accessing the organization's central repository or databases by means of global telecommunications. Both of these capabilities speed up the executive's business process and, more importantly for some sectors, give confidence to the trading partner that they have available all the knowledge with sufficient quality to complete the transaction. The building of relationships by sharing of information at the time of meeting is very important to the generation of alliances and partnerships. However, the security of storage in portable and easily removable devices is an issue for the information manager, as is the accessibility of global telecommunications of sufficient quality in some parts of the world. These problems will be overcome in time, but at present need to be attended to on a case by case basis.

Increasingly, the number of forms in which information needs to be exchanged is growing; it is now common for trading partners to request information in the form of text, sound, image and video. While these formats have been separately available for some time, their integration into a single channel of information exchange allows integrated tools to be used to manipulate them. Distinctions between broadcasting and transactions will be broken down as regulatory constraints are removed, and multimedia capabilities become available on all workstations. The management of this multimedia environment poses some new and formidable challenges and these are discussed in later sections.

A new variation on an old problem of information management comes with the speed of transmission of information over telecommunications networks; timestamping is used as a control mechanism for a number of purposes in a range of business sectors. When paper documents take hours or days to reach their destinations, there have been no problems of timestamping. Minute accuracy was good enough. With electronic transmissions at 155 Mbits.sec^{-1} rapidly becoming available in the US and Europe, times of arrival of documents and transactions may have to be recorded to microsecond accuracy, partly to provide proof of arrival times to third parties who are responsible for audits and partly to ensure causal relationships between different but connected elements of processes. It may be necessary to implement the desired controls in the processes in some other way to avoid such technological overheads. However, speed of response is vital and valuable to a number of organizations, dealers in commodities and international currency being the most obvious, and these controls must not be allowed to stand in the way of achieving the very small latency times that they require.

CREATION OF INFORMATION

The management of the original act of the creation of information is vital to all subsequent phases of information management. There are a number of factors to consider; in what format and medium has the information been represented? What tool set has the creator used and has this restricted or modified the creation process in a detrimental way? If the manager of the information environment has any control over the environment in which information is created should they take steps to ensure that it is as conducive as possible to high-quality creative processes? How does the creator ensure that, if the process is collaborative, then the technical environment is optimized to obtain the full benefits from the collaboration? Solutions to these problems include ensuring that 'authors' have available a wide range of multimedia authoring tools, that they work in the physical environment best suited to them, be that in an office, at home or in a studio, and that when working with others, the group-working environment that supports the authoring tools is as transparent and easy to use as possible.

Almost all newly created information will be integrated with pre-existing information. Continuity of choice of format and media standards will allow this process to be carried out easily and efficiently; where format conversions are necessary (a common example is between different word processing packages), tools for carrying out such conversions need to be well tested on realistic data and off-line, before implementing them as part of the enterprise's processes.

An integrated document, as a piece of information, may have a number of authors. Assignment to the appropriate author of a particular section or set of 'objects' may be needed for legal reasons. Traceability of source material will be necessary as an integral part of the information management process.

In all cases it will be necessary, where the information has some legal status, or needs to be traced as part of an indexing or workflow activity, for a number of labels to be bound to the document. The strength of this binding process needs to be sufficient for the purpose. For indexing an internal memo, including a field in the document that includes author's name and the filename where it is stored will probably be sufficient. Where it is a legally binding contract between two or more multinational organizations to build, say, a tunnel under the Bering Strait, it will be necessary to go to great lengths to ensure that no one can alter any part of any document or claim or deny authorship. Few standards in the electronic world exist as yet to handle this extreme situation, although they are being worked upon.

OWNERSHIP

The sharing of information is critical to the success of any enterprise built around information-based processes. As an asset information may be perceived as being originated by an individual acting as a private citizen or performing a role in an organization. Sometimes the words 'foreground' and 'background' information are used to describe these two types of information. Unless it is clear which is which, contracts of employment, dismissal cases, breach of contract suits and royalty benefits cannot be managed easily. This is not to suggest that this is an easy topic to manage. An individual's employability is directly affected by what they 'know'. If that 'knowledge' is regarded as the organization's property, they run the risk of attempting to deny rights of employment to the individual concerned, which in Europe at least is illegal. If on the other hand they take no steps to separate what is the organization's information and what is 'owned' by the individual, they are not protecting their information asset and could be accused of negligence by their shareholders.

It is not the subject of this chapter to discuss the legal aspects of employment conditions, contracts etc. Suffice to say that unless explicit discussion takes place about ownership and it is made clear, as far as possible, who owns what in information terms and, as important, if it cannot be made clear, what the policies of all parties are, little or no benefit will come from information sharing inside the organization. The pragmatic approach is to suggest that all things that are to do with specific processes and information pertinent to the enterprise belong to the enterprise, and the enterprise decides on the policy of release to third parties. All other information is common between the employee and the enterprise and can be used, within the constraints of the employment contract, by both parties to their individual benefit.

Indexes to information are prime information assets of an enterprise. They allow the information to be efficiently and effectively used. They may exist in a number of forms, both electronic and non-electronic. They may be held in the head of an employee. This may be a deliberate act to render the employee irreplaceable; the existence of that index in their head may not be common knowledge. The non-sharing of critical retrieval processes is one of the most common forms of using information as an instrument of personal power. Storekeepers who 'know where to find things' are classic example. This is not to say that they are not efficient in their job. It is to say, however, that they could not be integrated into a business process unless they disclosed, and indeed shared, how they carried out their activities.

Thus in improving or redesigning information management processes it is vital to discover all the 'hidden' processes that allow easy retrieval of information. In addition, as critical factors in allowing information to be used, configuration and revision controls need to be very rigorously applied to indexes and catalogues to ensure that they are accurate, up to date and not open to unauthorized modification, or even worse, destruction. Directories for electronic mail, group working and information sharing are a particularly important example of such a catalogue.

Some information may be regarded as confidential, either by the creator or by the enterprise. Standards for labels that can be bound to such information in such a way that allows the proper level of protection to be afforded to it are not available outside the Government, although there are a number of moves to create such standards. Labelling for this purpose forms part of the information management security policy that, in turn, is part of the overall information security policy of the enterprise.

STORAGE AND RETRIEVAL

The increased use of distributed information systems results in information being stored in the locality best suited to the systems manager but available to users wherever and whenever they need it. Users demand geographic independence in order to carry out their job. From an information management viewpoint this has a number of consequences. The interface for retrieval and storage needs to be identical for all applications and functions. Users can therefore navigate their way into and around information bases in a media- and location-independent way.

The networks that deliver the information from wherever it is stored to where the user needs it should also be uniform in the properties that the user sees, such as speed of response, integrity, addresses for messaging etc. These 'quality of service' issues that affect the quality of information management achieved by users are not always under the control of the enterprises supplying the overall capability. Outsourcing of telecommunications services is now quite common, and IS outsourcing is becoming more common. The quality of information management that derives from these services is then bound into the service contracts entered into by the parties concerned. It is essential that this service agreement is reached at the information level and not only at the data level. Most users will only be concerned with processes at the information level and will be detrimentally affected if the information management process is affected by changes in data management.

The volumes of information that need to be stored, how, by whom, where they are to be archived and whether or not redundant on-line storage is needed are an integral part of any information management process. While data compression technology makes only a passing difference for textual information in PCs, as far as multimedia is concerned, data compression algorithms could be the difference between success and failure for a number of information management processes. Integrating the storage, retrieval and archive strategies for the enterprise allows optimal tradeoffs between technologies and user requirements. However, this is not always how such matters are organized, usually because information repositories are not regarded as corporate assets, but more as departmental assets.

Most users wish to be assured that when they retrieve a piece of information it has not been altered since they or its creator stored it or if it has, that the change records are available to them. Integrity controls and methods are well understood and more easily implemented now thanks to new distributed environment management tools becoming available. However, a policy for such processes is required and needs to be understood by all users sharing information.

In addition, the access privileges to information are the critical element of the information management process that distinguishes unlimited access to everything by all from the desirable scenario of controlled access to those elements of information necessary for someone to carry out their role in the organization The policy for such access control stems from the description of the business processes and the information bases to which each role holder in the process has access. If it is included in the business process analysis, controlled information management within the context of the redesigned business process results.

MANIPULATION

The manipulation of information is a key part of the management process. It is the stage at which value can be added or subtracted from the existing information base. Creative activity that results in the product being more valuable than the starting information is the primary objective. Not excluded from this is the process by which a user merely reads and memorizes information stored in a computer system. This process adds to his knowledge base and allows him to make judgements that he would otherwise be less well equipped to make. The tools and equipment that are needed for such processes range from a simple standalone laptop PC on which sales figures have been entered, through to multimedia interactive workstations on-line to globally distributed information bases located on servers anywhere in the world.

The software that allows such manipulations to occur are becoming increasingly intuitive, and modern hypertext search tools allow very quick access via structured search processes or free text search algorithms. Sound and video embedded in 'documents' are recent extensions to the range of output media available. However, the ability to browse and flick through a document as intuitively as is possible with paper is not yet available from electronic sources. The printer will be with us for some time yet! The input media are becoming more diverse and pen-based input devices do allow a more traditional approach; they are not yet mature enough for a lot of applications, but it must be expected that they will become so.

The integration of multimedia source material is only just becoming possible as standards for data representation are becoming available. In addition sources of material in image and video in particular have a problem with control over copyright. Until this is resolved via digital signatures being embedded into images or some other protective mechanism applied, the sources of image-based information see little economic benefit accruing from the use of multimedia integration. Indeed the whole issue of copy (and destruction) control is fraught with difficulties in the electronic arena, not least because standards for labelling with copy numbers and for strong binding processes to prevent counterfeiting are not in place.

Concurrent working is often lauded as one of the advantages of electronic manipulation of information. It is difficult to perceive how two or more people can work on one file of paper-based information simultaneously. However, it is possible to see that possibility for electronically stored information. Integrity controls, conflict resolution and workflow management are the disciplines that have to be put in place to allow it to happen. Policy controls on changing the processes *per se* have to be in place to ensure that no inadvertent modifications are made to processes that contain concurrent working, thus jeopardizing their integrity.

COMMUNICATION

Directory controls as the key element of the communications process of information management processes have already been touched upon. Dividing the address space into domains allows the address information to be managed and controlled in a business process-oriented way, and integrated with the manipulation and storage and retrieval mechanisms.[3]

Informal and formal communications both have their place in an organization and need to be accommodated within the information management policy. Informal communications consist of messages and information transfers that do not commit the organization to a legally binding relationship (for example a contract, a purchase order) or the setting up of an internal policy binding on all or some of its members (for example pension fund arrangements, terms of employment, financial delegation). A formal communication does commit the organization in these areas.

The management of 'information that is being communicated' implies certain rights of users to communicate information when it is within the scope of the organizational communications policy for them to do so. It is also their duty not to carry out acts that transgress such policies. These statements may sound doctrinaire. Unless they are explicitly stated within an organization, information will be mismanaged and abused by users, not necessarily maliciously but because, by not stating clearly the rights and duties of the organization and its employees, no constraints would be applied to the communication of information. A blanket embargo is usually put on any communication in every employee's terms of employment; this is then relaxed by 'line managers' to cope with alliances and joint projects. In a loose network of virtual corporations it is not clear that this approach would work, and it is expected that more positive statements about each virtual team will be needed. Again, such activities and statements would be greatly facilitated by information being labelled more explicitly, as would the handling of the communications element of the information management security policy.

MIGRATION

The move from a centralized legacy system based around a mainframe or cluster of minicomputers is a common information management problem. The target architecture of a larger number of smaller servers to provide a better match to the business processes is assumed to provide easier management of the overall environment and to offer the flexibility that users need. Experience is showing that the flexibility is certainly being provided but, unfortunately, without good information management policies this flexibility can lead to anarchy. The mere inflexibility of mainframe systems led to good information management by default. Now it has to be designed. The 'easier to manage' benefits are yet to be realized also, since although the server systems themselves are easier to manage, the network that connects them together is not. It is the whole environment that delivers the geographic independence and flexibility that users need, and until enterprise system-wide management becomes available, the robustness of the information management policies and practices which depend upon them will be undermined. However, all the major vendors of products that are being used in distributed information systems are bringing out products that indicate a recognition of this particular requirement.

As part of the BPR process it must be recognized that legacy tasks and their associated systems will be removed. In addition new roles will be created within the new processes that will need to be populated by appropriately skilled and trained staff. These should be identified as early as possible and the systems and roles piloted to minimize the integration risks. During the introduction of the new processes, a transition planning team is essential and should not form part of old processes, or even new ones. The BPR implementation should be managed as a project in its own right with a dedicated project manager. Communications about the changes at all levels should be coherent and consistent and always come directly from the BPR team. All other staff are involved in the change in some way and have a vested interest, not necessarily conscious, in modifying the message about the BPR activities.

The change management process needs to be consistent and continuous. Information about the change process should be managed just like any other internal information and disseminated appropriately from the BPR team. The more 'special' it becomes, the more resistance to it is likely. Implementation of BPR is a special case of information management, even when the process to which the redesign is being applied is an information management process itself. However, the principles of information management should be applied to it just like any other process.

CONCLUSIONS

The integration of information managers, business process analysis and systems analysis will result in new roles in organizations, with the benefit that systematic approaches to businesses can be applied to all aspects of business where it is appropriate to do so. It must be clearly recognized that there are aspects where such an approach will not be appropriate, especially where the information content of the process has a large extrinsic component.

As a result of implementing BPR in the context of coherent information management it is likely that new roles for, example, for indexers, archivists, and process controllers, will be created and that traditional roles for, example, for registry clerks, operators, and supervisors, may disappear. The education and training consequences are profound and urgently need attention.

The restructuring of the IS industry is already happening. Increasingly firms are positioning themselves to supply solutions to user enterprises rather than products. Not that products are not needed; they are supplied to solution providers. Solution providers combine consultancy, system integrators and support. It is not yet clear whether the market will sustain such a business sector. The long awaited integration of the telecommunications industry and the information systems industry does seem a little closer, as the IS industry is now trying to exploit the bandwidth potential of the infrastructure of telecommunications service providers by pushing multimedia over wide area networks. However, it is still true that from a corporate information management viewpoint, the major problem to be solved is still perceived to be that of finding one telecommunications service provider that will, or is allowed to, give a one-stop shop, global service to support global information management.

Flexibility in information management processes comes as much from the will to make them flexible as from the technology that supports them. It comes from a recognition that people like to be involved in a process more than they like doing a task. The will to make these changes comes from the strategists in organizations, usually referred to as 'the top'. This might not be the case, and it is the author's experience that it is worth the time and trouble to talk to all staff in an organization to assess what their views might be on possible strategies for new processes.

The tools to analyse information management processes are becoming available, via either the BPR initiatives or from the use of workflow and groupware software to implement the new approaches, or simulation. What is needed still is a greater degree of professionalization of such methods to ensure their reliability. Enterprises are 'betting their business' on these re-engineered processes and they need reassurance that the work of implementing them is being carried out in accord with some professional standards.

Education and training for all people involved in information management will become essential. We are living in an information age and it is now impossible to conceive of anybody at school age not being taught the principles of information management. We are bombarded with information, both professionally and privately, and being able to cope with it successfully is an essential skill of the next millennium, just like swordsmanship was for a sizeable fraction of the current one; we have not needed that skill only in the last two centuries or so.

NOTES

1   The concept of managed objects, that is, all the entities that comply with the process management policy, be they people, machinery, processors, memory, internal processes, communications links or databases, is a powerful aid to describing process decomposition.

2   See Peter G.W. Keen (1991), *Shaping the Future: Business Design through Information Technology*, Cambridge, MA: Harvard Business School Press.

3   B.S. Collins and E.J. Humphreys (1994), 'An Overview of Security Domains', *DATAPRO: Information and Workflow Analyst*.

8 Problems and constraints

Peter Vickers

In this chapter, Peter Vickers, one of the founders of information management in the UK, and a highly skilled and experienced researcher and consultant, reviews problems and constraints. He takes a hard look at the situation on the ground from the standpoint of a man who for most of his career has 'been there, doing that', and illustrates that this field is not a cosy nook in the business organization.

He highlights the people problems of information management, from the 'information is power' problem to that of change management in the context of the introduction of major new systems and/or working methods.

The chapter then explores, through several brief case studies, the interaction between people and their information in a range of organizational settings. After discussing a range of technological problems, the chapter concludes with a look forward at the future of IM in terms of what needs to be done to accelerate the recognition and acceptance of the discipline, including the need for some kind of unifying framework, improved training and, ironically, better information about IM itself – doctor, heal thyself?

THE CONSULTANT'S VIEWPOINT

The aim of this chapter is to identify and discuss the reasons why, despite all that has been written about it, and the earnest endeavours of many experts and consultants, information management is still not taken as seriously as one might wish, and is still a long way from being universally accepted as a vital element of good management practice. Or to put it another way, if information management is such a good thing, why are so few organizations applying it?

Chapter 1 gave a broad definition of IM that can be taken to embrace all the operational activities that come within its scope, which might include anything from filing papers in alphabetical order to setting up a database on a computer. It is not my intention in this chapter to review all the problems that can afflict specific operations or the technology that supports them – that would make another book. My concern here is with problems and constraints affecting the actual process of management and the introduction of IM into organizations of various kinds.

The need for corporate IM, and the problems associated with introducing it, were brought home to me through project experience in my early years as a consultant with Aslib. Then as now, people within organizations would ask us to advise on how to improve or set up specific information systems or services, such as a new technical library, a departmental filing system, or a retrieval system for a collection of internally generated information. We were always working from the bottom up, tackling the problems of specific services and systems, and trying wherever possible to enlighten higher management about the wider context.

In nearly every case, it was evident that however brilliantly we, the consultants, advised the client on the design and operation of a particular system, it would not work properly or satisfy its users for long unless it could be made compatible with other systems and could be shown to support organizational objectives. This impasse could only be properly resolved if we were able to upgrade the status of the project, and be given the authority to study other information systems within the organization, which of course would mean involving successively higher levels of management in what had probably been seen at the outset as a relatively trivial exercise. Needless to say, we were not always successful in gaining access to these stratospheric levels of authority. We were after all information specialists, not management consultants. And anyway, IM had not yet been invented in the early 1970s.

A good example from those days is our experience with a certain international agency in Geneva, where we were initially asked by the then chief librarian to advise on a strategy for the future development of his library's services, which were in fact quite advanced in terms of its computer systems. It transpired, however, that in addition to this large, well-equipped central library there were some 20 other libraries of various sizes scattered through different departments of the organization. All the departmental heads had to be drawn into the project, so that we could investigate all these other resources and their relationship with the central library. We learned that these resources included units that were responsible for various kinds of operational information, such as training materials, statistics, and member country information, all of which was part of the wider picture to be considered in planning any future strategy for integrated information handling. But to make significant changes, it was necessary to involve the highest levels of management. In this case, such involvement was possible, because this was an organization whose entire activity was largely concerned with the processing of information in one way or another; its value was regarded objectively, and not in relation to a manufactured product. As a result of this project, systems were changed, attitudes were modified, networks were established, staff were retrained, and substantial improvements were achieved, but it all took a long time.

An example of what happens if the backing of top management is not obtained at the outset is shown by our experience, about 15 years ago, in carrying out a review of information services for a nationalized industry with research centres in several locations around the country. Our final report *129* proposed various measures for integrating these services, improving their systems, and generally raising their standards and their cost-effectiveness – all of which were endorsed by the manager who had initiated the project. The irascible research director to whom we had finally to present the report took a dim view of all this high-powered advice, however. 'What I wanted you to do was to tell us how to reduce our expenditure on books', he told us, rather forcefully.

From a consultant's point of view, IM presents a series of distinct challenges:

- *Diagnostic challenges*. These result from the tendency to ask the consultant to treat symptoms rather than the real information problems within an organization.
- *Organisational challenges*. The difficulty of convincing management of the need to tackle IM at the highest possible level, and that this may call for major changes in the way that the organization is run.
- *Methodological challenges*. The shortage of efficient and credible methods for investigating organizational requirements, including detailed information audits and analysis of information flows is not helping here (see also Chapter 4).
- *Systems design challenges*. The need for techniques to design, implement and integrate systems to support organization-wide IM.
- *Change management challenges*. Implementing IM may call for radical restructuring of the organization, and for fostering different attitudes among managers and staff towards information handling.

So much for the consultant's viewpoint. The remainder of this chapter is concerned with IM problems and constraints as they impinge upon the world at large. They will be considered under the headings of conceptual problems, people problems, problems with organizations and their management and, finally, technological problems.

THE DANGERS OF GENERALIZATION

Before we get into the main substance of this chapter, it is necessary to issue a government health warning about the dangers of generalization in this subject area. All too often, serious discussions on IM and related topics get impeded because of the tendency to over-generalize. The first thing to remember is that there are many different kinds of information, and they come in many different shapes and sizes; their value to different people in different situations may vary widely. The problems of implementing and practising good IM also vary a great deal depending on the size and type of organization that is concerned. It is frequently forgotten that IM is important for small and medium-sized organizations, as well as large corporations; and it matters to non-profit organizations as well as to multi-million-pound businesses. Last but not least, the relative importance of information management, just as for other basic resources, is different for different people within any organization. Any IM problem therefore needs to be studied with all these different viewpoints and parameters in mind.

There is a tendency for the term 'information management' to be applied without discrimination to all the constituent elements of the subject so that, for example, we see various advertisements proclaiming that all IM problems can be solved by the application of optical storage, networks, word processing, personal information managers, fuzzy searching, or any other new technique that is in fashion. This devalues the real subject and causes total bafflement to the lay public. IM will never achieve maturity as a discipline until a proper taxonomy of the subject has been established, and this should be a priority objective for its practitioners.

CONCEPTUAL PROBLEMS

One of the worst problems that plagues IM and impedes its wider recognition is the lack of any agreed definition of what it covers and of its relationship with information technology (with which it is all too often confused). This situation seems to be getting worse rather than better at present, as more and more people discover principles of IM for themselves and become convinced that *their* perception of the subject is better than any other. This naturally causes difficulties when they wish to discuss it with their colleagues.

One way of defining IM is by analogy with financial management. It is concerned with the management of information resources, in much the same way as the latter is concerned with the management of money. Financial management is a complex subject, involving many complex techniques, but people understand what it is about, because they are familiar with the concept of money. IM fails to gain such universal understanding because information is a more diffuse concept. One £10 note is worth the same as any other £10 note; a record containing information may be worth a fortune to one person, and nothing to another.

Associated with the confusion over the definition of IM is the job title 'Information Manager'. Assorted players in the information theatre had for a long time been looking for a designation that would help to elevate their prestige, or give them a better image. Along came the title of information manager, and everyone wanted to use it – information scientists, librarians, documentalists, computer managers and telecommunications specialists.

Which leads us to the question of what kind of information we are talking about. Many information managers of the information science/librarianship persuasion think of IM primarily in terms of the literature – that is, documents (mainly published) containing descriptive, qualitative information. Who can blame them? – the management of this kind of information alone is complicated enough. Others would extend the scope of IM to cover all textual material including all kinds of documents generated within an organization, such as correspondence, committee papers, personnel records, specifications, design documents and reports. A still wider definition includes transactional records of all kinds: orders, invoices, accounts, budgets, production records, and so on. At the far end of the spectrum, the definition would embrace all kinds of information, whether recorded or not, so that the field of communications would be subsumed within information management.

Another massive barrier to the recognition of IM is the difficulty of demonstrating the value of information. Information cannot be seen as a true 'good', to be bought and sold, because of its curiously transferable nature. Whatever value it *might* have in particular circumstances cannot be measured as conclusively as that of other basic resources. If a manufacturing firm has no materials or staff to make products, it can do nothing. If it has no information it may not be very efficient or competitive but it can usually still function.

However widely the notion is accepted that information is a primary resource, the truth is that it seldom rates the same level of priority as money, materials or the workforce. Many senior managers in industry today recognize the importance of good information management but, when it comes to the crunch in a contest for investment, activities which directly and visibly support the production process and bring in revenue will always win.

This view of priorities is not true, of course, for organizations whose business is to process or sell information, such as database producers, professional associations, government departments or international agencies. Indeed, it is encouraging to note that the UK Government (or parts of it, at least) has shown keen awareness of the need for IM within its departments. The CCTA publication *Managing Information as a Resource*[1] is an excellent introduction to the subject, containing useful practical guidance on how to apply good IM. It would be interesting to know how widely it has been read and acted upon since it was published in 1990.

Proving the value of IM is no easier than proving the value of information. Many have tried to come up with ways of proving the benefit, in financial terms, that corporate IM can bring to an organization. Alas, none has yet succeeded. (Some benchmarking projects have been privately commissioned but the results are not as yet in the public domain, Ed.)

These conceptual problems seriously impede the development of IM as a professional discipline. It is the responsibility of researchers, consultants, teachers and practitioners to resolve them if IM is ever to achieve the recognition and status that it warrants.

PEOPLE PROBLEMS

Just as in other walks of life, it can be said of IM that it would be much easier to apply if only it didn't involve people – and that includes the people who generate information, those who use it, and those who manage information handling operations.

The worst thing about people, from a system designer's viewpoint, is that they are all different. It follows that one of the main barriers to wider acceptance of the need for IM is the diversity of individual attitudes and information gathering habits in the workplace. In organizations of all types (research, manufacturing, service industry, government department, etc.), we find some people who expect to have information services provided for them, and others who prefer the DIY approach, insisting that only they know what they want and how best to exploit the sources available. This anarchic behaviour is generally accepted in a way that would be unthinkable in the case of other basic resources. The diversity of information user types was explored in detail in studies of research organizations by T.J. Allen[2] and others in the 1970s, and this work is worth revisiting in relation to the development of IM.

A more specific people-problem is that of the Philistines who are found in many organizations. There is a strong tradition (especially in the UK) of using the 'old boy' and other informal networks as information sources, rather than formal sources, particularly for business information. This attitude is particularly prevalent in small businesses, but is not unknown in the larger corporations, and is generally inhospitable to any suggestion of IM. Its proponents resist the notion that information handling needs to be formalized, claiming that 'everything I need to know I either keep in my head, or I can get from my friend down the road'. Government initiatives in recent years to provide better information services to small businesses have repeatedly met this problem of persuading the potential clientele that, if properly used, information can help them to become more profitable and more secure in the marketplace. Yet if these small business managers cannot appreciate the potential value of information, they are unlikely to be convinced of the need for IM. We can only hope that these attitudes will be altered in the wake of changes in educational methods, which now tend to encourage greater use of formal information sources than was the case a generation ago.

Many of the problems affecting IM spring from the relative newness of the subject. The majority of those directly involved in IM have seen it evolve over the past 15 years; they come from a variety of professional backgrounds. There is a shortage of managers who really understand its significance. The teaching of IM, now almost exclusively the province of business studies departments, is far from standardized in its content and emphasis and there is a shortage of people with a common view of the subject to teach it. There are not yet enough experts who really understand IM and who can advise capably on its application in all kinds of organizations. It is to be hoped that this situation will improve over the coming years as more people with broad training and experience in IM rise to senior positions. The professions involved in IM must keep up the pressure to improve the quality of training for future workers in this field, so that they are equipped to face its challenges.

PROBLEMS WITH ORGANIZATIONS AND THEIR MANAGEMENT

It is an interesting exercise to consider how you might apply IM to yourself. Start with an information audit. Think of all the information resources available to you in your working and leisure life. If you are a white-collar worker, the former might include the papers in and on your desk, the information held on your PC, the filing system in your office, maybe a company information service of some kind, various external sources including perhaps your professional society, a chamber of commerce, or a trade association. In your leisure/domestic life, your resources would include your home filing system for bills, insurances, agreements, income tax papers, and other correspondence, your telephone and address lists, personal library and so on.

How might you optimize the way you use all these resources? Would your quality of life be improved if you could learn ways to exploit these resources more effectively? Would you benefit by some form of personal IM, perhaps calling for the adoption of a planned regime for the collection and use of all the information you need in your life?

As noted earlier, people are very much a variable quantity, so while some people would find this an interesting question, others would find it totally boring. Organizations are populated with people of all these kinds, with widely differing attitudes towards information and its use. No wonder it is so difficult to apply perfect IM. And no wonder it is not easy to convince top management that IM will bring untold benefits to their organization, in return for the upheaval that its introduction may impose. The degree of motivation for making a corporate commitment to IM is bound to vary enormously, depending on the kind of organization concerned.

The case for IM is further weakened by a lack of understanding of the relationship between IM and other aspects of management, such as planning and operational control. There is general agreement that better information provision for top management will substantially improve an organization's performance and success in the marketplace, and many organizations have invested or are investing in sophisticated executive information systems which provide seamless access to all kinds of information. But it seems that little is known about just how great a benefit such systems can achieve, and the designers of these systems tend to be more concerned with the technology needed to handle the information than with how the system will actually be integrated with the management process. This is yet another indication that IM is a vast subject which needs to be explored and studied by people who are not motivated mainly by market forces.

It has been pointed out in a recent research report[3] that 'As the nature and use of corporate information changes, the associated planning and control processes must also evolve'. Good IM should theoretically open the way for better management strategies, which in turn will lead to new information requirements, including better methods of presenting information, which will suggest new approaches to IM, and so on and so on. Similarly, good IM should enable the workforce as a whole to function more effectively, especially (but not exclusively) where their work involves information processing of any kind. The style of IM must evolve to meet the changing requirements that will result from changing practices.

IM should be concerned with optimizing the flow of all kinds of information within and between organizations. The flow of information is closely linked to organizational structure, so the introduction of corporate IM can often mean radical changes to the organization. Early examples of this appeared in the early 1980s, particularly in the US, where many organizations appointed chief information officers (CIOs) who were given responsibility for all information functions including computer systems, telecommunications, information services and records management.[4] The basic organizational structure for IM then proposed was of the form:

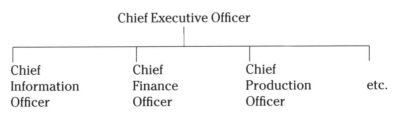

Chief Executive Officer

Chief Information Officer   Chief Finance Officer   Chief Production Officer   etc.

This was a practical arrangement for medium- to large-sized industrial firms, but was not suitable for smaller firms (which could not afford so many executives), nor for many non-manufacturing organizations, nor for large, group-based firms where the picture gets more complicated, with various permutations of the way in which functions are divided between group and divisional level. The problem in all this lies in determining optimum structures for information flow in different types of organization.

In 1982, the Aslib Consultancy Service was commissioned to carry out a study of information flow between the DHSS and the NHS, and within the NHS, and to advise on a strategy for introducing appropriate information technology to improve these flows where necessary.[5] This study highlighted the enormous complexity of information flows within a structure comprising several levels – the DHSS, the 14 Regional Health Authorities, and the 193 District Health Authorities – each of which had its own complex internal structure and its own systems for processing, storing and retrieving information. Each level moreover exchanged information with the outside world (BMA, local authorities, FPCs, CHCs, the press, etc.) through a multitude of channels.

Even with the limited opportunity we had to examine information systems in any detail at each level it was evident then that there was a need for better IM within the NHS, especially to improve the handling of management information in its vertical flow through the structure (which was in fact being tackled concurrently by the Körner Committee). Better IM was also needed at each level, but the Regional and District Health Authorities and the individual hospitals and clinics all have a large degree of autonomy, and it would have been no easy matter to introduce any kind of overall IM policy or practice that they would all accept. As was and is so often the case, there was a policy regarding the provision of computer support within each region, but no such policy governing information resources.

Analogous situations arise in other Government departments, and the problems which arise tend to be very complex. The fact is that although some people can do a fairly good job of solving IM problems within a single self-contained organization, even the cleverest of us can find it difficult to cope when trying to optimize the design and operation of information systems or networks on a national or international scale, where interdependencies and interactions become very complex. We can manage the technology (most of the time) and the organization of knowledge (ditto), but we are not very good at dealing with people and organizations in this context. We lack the necessary methodology for investigating and analysing these situations, and we lack proper understanding of the fundamental principles of individual and social behaviour involved in information use. As pointed out earlier, there is a serious need for more research in this field.

To take another example, the Employment Department supports, via the Training and Enterprise Councils, over 80 Training Access Points (TAPs) which maintain local databases of information about vocational education and training courses, to make it easy for people to find out about the training opportunities that are available to them. The information for these databases has to be regularly collected and updated from training providers of all kinds – universities, colleges, commercial training specialists, and so on. The same providers get an average of up to ten requests for the same information, in various different formats, from other database providers and directory publishers, and get rather fed up about this. In the interests of good IM, of course, it would be much better if the information could be collected just once and used by all.

In 1988, we helped to carry out a study of the databases supported by public funds in this field, which included local TAP databases and several databases with national coverage. The aim was to recommend a strategy to achieve coherence between, and compatibility of, such databases. One of the outcomes from this work was the development of a set of agreed database standards, which have now been widely adopted. The problem of multiple data collection has still not been resolved, however, mainly because the commercial database providers operate on a different data collection cycle from the TAPs, and the TAPs have not shown themselves collectively to be able to meet the standards of data collection required by the commercial firms. This illustrates the difficulty of applying IM on a large scale, particularly where several different organizations are involved which have different objectives and priorities, and which are not subject to a single authority. Good IM calls for the introduction of standards, but these cannot work unless there is some means for enforcing them.

The introduction of corporate IM and the development of integrated systems raise issues of information ownership which never surfaced in the pre-IM era. At the simplest level, if it is suggested that databases of specialized information collected by individuals or groups are made generally accessible on the corporate local area network (LAN), the 'owners' of the information may feel that this will erode their status as experts, and will resist accordingly. Problems of a different kind arise with respect to information bought in from external sources, which is usually subject to licence agreements which lay down a limit to the number of users. This issue is of growing concern in the field of electronic publishing, where the rights of authors and publishers will eventually need to be redefined in this new context; any new principles which emerge may well be applicable also in the context of corporate IM.

One of the key problems of IM is how far to go? Should we be trying to redesign organizations and the way people work in order that they can handle information as effectively as possible, or should we concentrate on designing good systems to meet specific needs, and then try to integrate them so far as this is reasonable? Just as there is a wide difference between quality assurance and total quality management, there is an order-of-magnitude difference between incremental improvement of information handling and the implementation of full IM. A half-hearted approach would not be acceptable for financial management; is it good enough for information management? On the other hand, it is at the system level that the pain is generally felt when things go wrong. There is seldom a powerful enough impulse to take the strategic view and tackle the problem at the organizational level.

TECHNOLOGICAL PROBLEMS

Probably the greatest technological problem affecting IM is that there is so much technology about, and it keeps changing very rapidly. A big problem for information managers is that of achieving any kind of stable condition in which to consolidate their systems development. Continually changing the technology to take advantage of improvements in processor speed or new versions of software packages can be counter-productive. Good IM means that any upgrading of systems should be done within the framework of careful strategic planning.

Technological problems are encountered in designing systems which can support corporate IM, the most difficult being those met with when attempting to develop an integrated information system, which has recently been defined[6] as one having the following properties:

1   It provides any authorized user in the organization with the capability to access all data or information necessary to support the business process and allows the fulfilment of organization goals and objectives.
2   It is available at any location within the organization.
3   It presents information or data in a suitable form and quality to enable the user to work at maximum efficiency in achieving the organizational goals and objectives.

The technological problems of integration are, however, considerably more easy to solve than those of adapting our ways of thinking and working to take full advantage of the 'perfect' access to information resources that IM should be aiming to provide. The cost of developing integrated systems is high and the ultimate benefit cannot be determined with certainty, so it is hardly surprising that management tends to move with caution in this area.

It is a matter for serious concern that many organizations still believe that all IM problems can be solved by technology alone, for example by the application of optical storage to solve all their document management problems. They are reluctant to accept (a) that detailed investigation of present information handling practices is necessary, and (b) that major management changes will be needed to implement such systems effectively. This causes problems for them and for the consultants they employ to make it all come right. The onus is on practitioners, teachers and consultants to get the message across to all managers that IM is not just another name for information technology, and that it has a much wider significance.

Whatever problems are caused by the technology, it has to be said in its defence that it has been instrumental in raising awareness of what is involved in managing information effectively. Attempts by individuals to set up their own databases on PCs or even to organize their word processor files often bring home some of the basic lessons of IM at the operational level, and do so more effectively than any formal training course could hope for.

THE FUTURE FOR IM

As a keen advocate of IM, I tend to deplore the blinkered attitudes still found in many organizations toward the notion of managing information as a resource, and their resistance to any suggestion that formal procedures should be   *137* established to achieve this. I have to admit, however, that a great deal of progress has been achieved over the past 15 years, and there are signs that this progress will be maintained. There are encouraging indications of growing government interest in the subject of IM, and a recognition of its significance in other quarters. In some ways, the increasing use of information technology makes it inevitable that some basic appreciation of the need for IM will take hold in the majority of organizations. The question is, what needs to be done to accelerate and consolidate this process?

Progress is hindered by the lack of scientifically derived fundamental principles on which to base the application of IM; all we have at present is a few management techniques, some bits of organizational theory, some fairly crude techniques for systems design, all held together with a little homespun information science and a certain amount of common sense. There is no kind of unified theory of IM.

There is a need for better methods of identifying organizational information requirements at all levels. Too often these requirements are determined by means of crude surveys where 'users' (which should mean all of us) are invited to articulate their information needs.

It is time to give up our empirical approach to IM and to treat it as a mature subject. As mentioned previously, there is a need for more research on the application of IM in all kinds of organizations, that goes beyond the case study approach. In particular, we need to gain a better understanding of the relationship between IM and other aspects of management.

The best base from which to undertake such research would surely be the business schools which teach the subject. But who would fund it? The British Library has initiated and funded useful IM projects in recent years, but what is needed here is a fairly ambitious programme that would overstretch their present resources. Since IM is of particular importance to industry, it would seem reasonable to suggest that industry should support research in this field – perhaps with a little help from the Department of Trade and Industry.

There is also a need for much more and better training in IM, for all types of managers, but the value of training will continue to be limited unless and until the subject has the solid foundation that only systematic study and research can provide.

One final problem, which cannot be ignored, is the appalling lack of good information resources on the subject of IM itself. This was brought home to me forcibly in the course of writing this chapter, when I discovered that the Science Reference and Information Service, within which the British Library's Business Information Service is based, does not hold the *International Journal of Information Management*! Searching on-line databases for IM literature can be a frustrating and expensive exercise. The relevant literature, in so far as it is captured by commercial databases, is scattered across *Library & Information Science Abstracts*, *Management Abstracts*, *Computer and Control Abstracts*, and *Electronic Publishing Abstracts*, but much falls down the cracks in between and gets lost. IM could take a great leap forward if only its advocates and practitioners established better IM in their own field.

NOTES

1   Central Computer and Telecommunications Agency (1990), *Managing Information as a Resource*, London: HMSO.

2   Allen, T.J. (1970), 'Roles in Technical Communication Networks', in C. Nelson, D. Pollock, et al., *Communication among Scientists and Engineers*, Lexington, MA: Heath, 191–208. See also McClure, C.R. (1978), 'The Information-Rich Employee and Information for Decision Making', *Information Processing and Management*, **14**, 381–94.

3   Brittain, M. (ed.) (1992), *Integrated Information Systems*, British Library R & D Report 6054, London: Taylor Graham Publishing.

4   There has been some suggestion recently that CIOs are a declining species. See Earl, M. and Vivian, P. (1993), *The Role of the Chief Information Officer*, London: London Business School.

5   NHS/DHSS Health Services Information Steering Group and NHS Computer Policy Committee (1983), *Introducing IT in the District Office*, London: The King's Fund.

6   Brittain, M. (ed.) (1992), *Integrated Information Systems*, British Library R&D Report 6054, London: Taylor Graham Publishing.

Part IV

A TRANSATLANTIC PERSPECTIVE

9   A Translatlantic perspective on information management

Blaise Cronin and Kara Overfelt

Here Blaise Cronin, formerly Principal Research Officer at Aslib in the UK, then professor at Strathcyde University before taking up his deanship at Indiana University, critically reviews the US experience, and, with his co-researcher Kara Overfelt, provides a masterly literature review of the field, in areas such as technology and the hybrid manager.

RECENT HISTORY

There is no one American view on information management; there are several. What strikes even the most casual observer is the wide range of cognate terms in vogue, and how loosely they seem to be used, in both the academic and professional press. The couplet 'information management' is truly chameleonic in character. Or, to be more charitable, we could say that information management is 'an emergent field of interest' (McGee and Prusak, 1993, p. 230).

And yet, Federal Government interest in information management can be traced back two decades to the time when Congress authorized creation of the Commission on Federal Paperwork in 1974. Another notable landmark was the passing of the Paperwork Reduction Act 1980, the goals of which included expanding and strengthening 'federal information management activities' and establishing 'a single focal point for information management within the Federal Government' (Horton and Marchand, 1982, p. 6). Federal Government policies have undergone fitful refinement since the 1980s, taking account of developments in electronic storage and distribution technologies, particularly as they affect citizen access to, and the pricing of, government information. The OMB's (Office of Management and Budget) Circular A-130, and rolling revisions thereof, provide a useful barometer of changes in both public opinion and public policy with regard to the management and exploitation of federal information resources.

In the UK, the Treasury, mindful of developments in the US, took a leadership role in promoting the concept of information management within central government. The culmination of its efforts was *Managing Information as a Resource*, which was intended to be a *vade mecum* for managers at all levels in government departments (CCTA, 1989) (to which Bill Cook, Chapter 6 was a leading contributor, Ed.).

The early 1980s also witnessed a flurry of interest in the application of information management concepts to the harnessing of distributed information and computing resources in the university sector. In the US, the National Library of Medicine supported the development of a number of integrated academic information management systems (IAIMS) initiatives, such as that at the University of Maryland (Ball and Douglas, 1988). Over time, the expansion of the IAIMS acronym altered to become integrated advanced information management systems, and expectations were scaled back as experience taught some of the pioneers that 'it usually takes at least ten years for a paradigm shift of this magnitude' (Ball and Reese, 1994, p. 326).

In the UK, a major restructuring of the National Health Service (NHS) catalysed interest in the application of information management methods and techniques in hospitals and primary health care centres throughout the country. The prime mover in developing systematic IM training initiatives was the Information Management Group, established by the NHS management executive (see Brittain and Abbott, 1993). This initiative seems to have had more enduring impact on IM thinking and practice than that of the Treasury.

ANCHOR DEFINITIONS

What does the journal literature have to say on the subject of information management? Until recently, an obvious starting point would have been *Information Management Review*, published by Aspen. The journal has, however, ceased, though whether this fact should be construed as a reflection on the robustness of the information management concept is debatable. But there are other US journals, magazines and newsletters to which we can turn for a sense of the burning issues and the prevailing consensus: *Information Strategy: The Executive's Journal*, *Information Systems Management*, *Journal of Information Systems* (a publication of the American Accounting Association), *Information Resources Management Journal*, and *CIO* (*The Magazine for Information Executives*) are obvious contenders.

Most of these carry an informative scope note or mission statement which can be used to draw a map of the intellectual terrain, and the extent to which boundary lines have been demarcated. *Information Resources Management Journal*, for instance, describes its mission in terms of developing and improving 'the theory and practice of information resources management' and educating 'organizations on how they can benefit from their information resources'. In line with this policy, the journal invites papers dealing with, *inter alia*, the management of human elements of information systems, the strategic use of information resources, and management utilization of information resources.

Information Strategy: The Executive's Journal has, as the subtitle suggests, a clear target audience in mind, and sees its focus squarely as the 'effective and strategic management of information systems'. There seems not to be any overlap in terms of advisory/editorial board memberships across these journals, which may suggest that the principals involved do indeed perceive their specialisms and products to be different in meaningful ways.

A systematic comparison of content and coverage in each of these journals would be revealing; even more so, a comparison which included the equivalent set of UK and European publications: journals such as the *International Journal of Information Management, Journal of Strategic Information Systems, European Journal of Information Systems, Journal of Information Technology* (published by the Association for Information Technology) and the magazine, *Managing Information* (published by the Association for Information Management).

For instance, *The International Journal of Information Management* provides a 'focus and source of up to date information on the developing field of information management', which it circumspectly chooses not to define: it does, however, welcome submissions in such areas as information systems, information overload, computer and telecommunications technologies, human communication and people in systems and organizations. Its stable mate, the *Journal of Strategic Information Systems*, nails its flag to the mast of 'intellectual rigor and practical experience' while, not unreasonably, emphasizing the 'need for IT systems to be driven by business requirements'. *Journal of Information Technology* deals with the 'many different applications and the impact of IT on organizations', but more specifically with topics such as corporate IS strategies, management of information systems development and implementation, and management practice in IT. The boundary lines between all of these, it must be said, appear fuzzy. Presumably, each of these journals, and other (marginal) titles, such as the *International Journal of Technology Management, Behaviour and Information Technology*, has a sense of its own purpose, market, and potential authors, and also a sense of what distinguishes it from the others. The reader, however, may not always be blessed with such a sense, as many articles could be effortlessly interchanged between these publications without noticeable loss of thematic coherence or credibility.

To some extent, these journals do deal with different issue sets, though perhaps it would be fairer to say that they deal with broadly similar themes, but at different levels of granularity. They have, however, little in common with their similarly named counterparts, *Information Systems* and *Information Processing & Management*, both of which have an essentially technical, as opposed to a strategic or business, perspective on the management of information technology, systems and resources. We would contend that this product confusion is a function of the wider conceptual and terminological confusion which continues to surround the concept of information management in the US (and, for that matter, elsewhere).

The confusion is not only at the inter-journal level; intra-journal uncertainties can also be detected. Reponen (1993, p. 100), writing in the *Journal of Strategic Information Systems*, maintains that the journal's contributors, and perhaps even its editors, 'have been a little confused about what is strategic and what is not'. He goes on to note that the concept of 'strategic information systems' has been widely used and has many different interpretations, including the following: strategic information technology, information systems strategy, information technology strategy, information management strategy, strategic information systems planning.

Terminological wrangling is not restricted to the US. In the launch issue of the *European Journal of Information Systems*, Boaden and Lockett (1991) asserted that IM (information management) was poised to see off contender labels, old and new (MIS, IS, IRM, IT, etc.), and set to become the preferred generic in the acronym-plagued information (studies) literature. To date, their prediction has not held up, at least as far as the North American scene is concerned. From Latin America, Paez-Urdaneta (1992, p. 47) proposes a less than lucid distinction between holistic IM ('the optimization of the information environment of organizations in the public and private sectors'), strategic IM ('the enhancement of the information value and impact of particular organizational functions') and information resources management ('the efficient administration of the organizations' information assets'), all of which merely serves to muddy the water even further.

INFORMATION RESOURCE(S) MANAGEMENT

Since definitions abound, where better to start than the Library of Congress subject heading list? Intriguingly, 'information management' does not feature, but 'information resources management' does, and is defined thus:

> Here are entered works on the coordination of information gathering and dissemination responsibilities within an organization. The concept combines under one management such traditional organizational functions as: ADP management, communication technology management, procurement, formulation of regulations standards, paperwork management, security, information systems development, data base management, and library and information services (Library of Congress Subject Headings, 1994, p. 2450).

The key to this working definition would seem to be co-ordination and collocation. But there is no explicit mention of the strategic dimension, which even the records management community, on both sides of the Atlantic, has now latched on to in its expansionist zeal.

A recent (UK) definition of records management runs as follows: 'a practice which allows the parent organization to gain the greatest efficiency and effectiveness from its information resources in an economical way, by the development of strategic processes and procedures to handle that information' (Jones, 1994, p. 14). By comparison with the best US rhetoric, however, this is fairly mild stuff. Dykeman (1992, p. 47) maintains that records management, more appropriately termed records and information management (RIM), 'is one of the most indispensable functions in business, government, or any other type of organization . . . While today's records management harnesses the power of every computer technology, RIM will be a priority concept long after the current hot technologies are mastered and assimilated under the organizational information systems umbrella.' But what exactly does the concept entail? According to the Association of Records Managers and Administrators

(ARMA) International, RIM is concerned with 'the planning, controlling, directing, organizing, training, promotion and other managerial activities involved with respect to records and information creation, maintenance and use and disposition'. Here again, catholicity is of the essence.

The blending of the terms 'information resource', 'management', 'information systems', 'business', 'strategic', 'information technology' continues apace throughout the global literature, and almost every possible permutation seems to have been tried.

And the mainstream academic world is no less whimsical in its anchoring of key curricular concepts. In a recent article, Quarstein et al. (1994, p. 63) argue that North American MBA programmes may be producing graduates with 'limited and perhaps insufficient knowledge and skills in IT'. They support their view with the results of a national survey, which leads them to propose a four-part IT syllabus for business schools. Part I, labelled 'Technology/ Development', includes such classic systems/software elements as database management, applications development, systems development and data communication. Part II, 'Applications Concepts', includes management information, decision support, office automation, expert systems and transaction processing. It is only with Part III, 'Information Resources Management', that the strategic and organizational dimensions come into play: IS for competitive advantage, strategic role of IS, data as a resource, organizational impact, business links to IS strategy, management of IS and measuring IS effectiveness. Part IV, 'Miscellaneous Topics' includes privacy and security, ethical issues, legal aspects of IS, ergonomics and health issues. Nowhere in the schematic do we find the term 'information management'.

Shah and Leja (1991, p. 30) have also weighed in with a definition of information resource management which sits quite comfortably alongside that used by Quarstein et al.: for them, IRM is a 'process that links business information needs to information system solutions by utilizing existing information technology and strategically adding or changing IT'. This, at least, makes explicit the connection between a company's business strategy and its information technology strategy, a point elaborated on by Reponen (1993, p. 102), who is particularly sensitive to business process re-engineering and information management issues: 'strategic planning of information systems is an interactive learning process for the creation of a strategy for business process redesign and development incorporating information technology. The strategy presents plans for information systems design, implementation and operation for this purpose.' Others are less bullish about IRM:

> There was a movement 10 or 15 years ago called information resources management (IRM). It's pretty much died out now, but one of its central tenets is that you're really out to manage in an innovative fashion libraries, records management, office automation and IS. One of the reasons IRM [nearly] died is that people view it as being self-serving for heads of data processing because they were the ones who were going to get this big pool of resources (Davenport, quoted in Maglitta, 1994a, p. 72).

THE CHIEF INFORMATION OFFICER

The emergence of the chief information officer (CIO) was celebrated in a 1986 *Business Week* cover story entitled 'Management's Newest Star: Meet the Chief Information Officer'. In a short time, chief information officer became the preferred title for those, typically on, or near, the vice presidential rung of the Fortune 500 corporate ladder, who had oversight responsibility for information systems and technology within the organization. The term seems to have been used first by Synnott and Gruber (1981, p. 66) to connote 'the senior executive responsible for establishing corporate information policy, standards, and management control over all corporate information resources'.

According to Strassmann (1990, p. 300) the 'basis of a CIO's power was the establishment of functional ("corporate" or "enterprise") information systems that transcended departmental boundaries'. All too often, however, the fanfare which greeted the appointment of a CIO to launch a long-term, enterprise-wide information management project was followed by '[w]asteful and costly skirmishes' placing the 'embattled CIO' in an 'untenable position'. All of which leads Strassmann to translate CIO as 'commanding impossible operations' (ibid. p. 301).

Stephens (1994, p. 48) is but one among many who have stressed the importance of closing the 'gap between the use of information resources and the strategic objectives of the firm' at a time of growing market competitiveness, domestically and globally. But there is another gap to be closed. In fact, managing the communication gap between CIOs and CEOs (chief executive officers) has become something of a leitmotif in the professional literature, or as Feeney et al. (1992, p. 435) put it, in the context of a UK-based survey, the need for 'top management involvement in the exploitation of information technology (IT) is a recurring theme of information management'. However, as is so often the case, we are left, tantalizingly, to wonder just what is meant by the term 'information management', since no firm definition is proffered by the authors.

In recent years, the pressures on CIOs have grown considerably, not least because of the difficulties of demonstrating credible returns on ever-increasing investments in IT, and this is reflected in the high turnover rate among senior IS professionals. Indeed, such are the challenges and uncertainties confronting many CIOs, as businesses work though complex restructuring and engineering exercises, that Laplante (1993, p. 56) has facetiously suggested translating CIO as 'career is over'. One of the main problems has been disagreement over priorities between CIOs and CEOs. This is nowhere better illustrated than in the two groups' prioritization of business process re-engineering (BPR). Laplante notes that 88 per cent of CEOs see business process re-engineering as critical to corporate competitiveness, a view shared by only 2 per cent of CIOs. Such divergence on a central issue certainly does not augur well for the future of the CIO.

And the problem goes deeper: it's not just CEOs and CIOs who are at loggerheads; COOs (chief operating officers) and CIOs are not always on the same wavelength either, and Menagh (1994, p. 87) calls this one of the 'political fault lines in today's corporations': COOs, who are often given responsibility for implementing business process re-engineering (BPR), have all too often under-involved the CIO. While Hammer states that IS cannot drive re-engineering efforts, he does acknowledge that they 'must be driven by top management' (quoted in Menagh, 1994, p. 87), which, presumably, should include all officers with the prefix 'chief' in their title. The CIOs' poor relationships with both COOs and CEOs may militate against their active participation in BPR, leading to a failure to fully appreciate its significance, and rendering them unlikely lead actors in business strategy planning and process re-engineering.

It can be instructive to contrast the uninhibited optimism of the 1986 *Business Week* article with later, more measured assessments of the CIO's contributions to corporate America. This 'information elite' was going to harness the strategic use of information and 'change the organization' (*Business Week*, 1986, pp.160, 172), and it was confidently expected that CIOs would 'proliferate in the next few years, especially in banking, financial services, airlines, and insurance – the most information-dependent businesses . . . it's a safe bet that there'll be more chief information officers on the scene in the years ahead'. Rifkin (1993, p. 96), however, paints a gloomy picture of turnover, attrition and downsizing in the CIO ranks. The average tenure for a CIO is now less than five years, and turnover is running at 20 per cent per annum. Chief information officers have the ignominious distinction of being fired at twice the rate of any other professional, which is quite a come-down for *Business Week*'s (1986, p. 160) vaunted 'Renaissance man'.

THE HYBRID MANAGER

Despite the dissonance between early promise and later reality, commentators, both then and now, agree strongly on the importance of combining technical know-how with business acumen in the CIO role model. As one of the CIOs quoted in the *Business Week* (1986, p. 162) article put it, the chief information officer post 'is not for the classic computer jock or machine-room honcho'. Instead, the CIO should be a strong communicator, straddle two camps (management and technology), have access to top management and concentrate on long-term strategy.

The importance of creating a new breed of hybrid information professional was also recognized in the UK. In 1990, the British Computer Society (BCS) produced a report which mapped out a strategy for producing a cadre of such hybrids – 'managers combining business understanding, technical competence and organizational knowledge and skills'. The authors of the study estimated that the UK would need to produce 10 000 hybrids by 1995 and suggested ways in which that goal might be attained. It is questionable, though, whether this early enthusiasm has translated into concrete actions on a scale, or of the consistency, necessary to bring the vision to life.

One problem seems to be the difficulty in actually finding individuals who possess, and can successfully apply, the portfolio of skills and knowledge associated with the ideal hybrid. As Ziskin of Ernst and Young (quoted in Maglitta, 1994b, p. 80) put it: 'The traditional [information technology] track is not preparing people for this position.' This is also the opinion of McFarlan (quoted in Rifkin, 1993, p. 101) who notes that most leaders in the IT field came to it 'with backgrounds in math, science or computer science and remain fasci-nated with technology'. Even more cynical is Ouellette (also quoted in Maglitta, 1994b, p. 81) who says that 'many traditional IS heads pay only lip service to team building, empowerment, Total Quality Management and other important practices'. He goes on to suggest that this leads many CEOs to 'teach business people technology' (ibid.) rather than the obverse. The poten-tial downside with this approach is that they run the risk of being deceived by technologically sophisticated subordinates.

Probably the most systematic specification of the paragon is that provided by Earl and Skyrme (1992, pp. 169). They sketch out the roles, responsibilities and competencies associated with a fully developed hybrid ('a breed of man-agers who blend information management skills with general management skills'), in the process toying with personality profiles and Myers Brigg Type Indicators. One detects, however, some category confusion, as the emergent hybrid subsumes three other roles, those of IT leaders, impresarios and professionals. However, the authors quickly check themselves with the cave at that the 'hybrid manager is a concept, a capacity for a role, a manage-ment development goal; it is not a job title or a description and will not be found in an organization chart' (ibid. p. 172). They conclude their paper with a discussion of the educational, recruitment, and career development implica-tions for this new breed of IT manager/entrepreneur, and a welcomingly realistic rider to the effect that 'creating hybrid managers is not, by itself, suffi-cient to develop a meaningful partnership between IS and business' (ibid. p. 184).

WIN SOME . . . LOSE SOME

Both the academic and business/professional literature are peppered with success tales and, less frequently (for obvious reasons), tales of woe describ-ing the genesis and outcomes of information systems installations, IRM initia-tives, and large-scale IT projects. One gets the sense from much of the popular trade press that 'information management' is treated as a synonym for 'infor-mation technology/information systems management'. There is little explicit reference to what might be termed 'total information' (Cronin and Davenport, 1991, p. 118). The fixation with information technology means that due con-sideration is not always given to the 'content and purpose aspects of infor-mation behaviour' (Roberts and Wilson, 1987, p. 68). It is clear that critical elements of the information mix are being ignored either because they historically have been taken for granted, or because they have been sourced from outside the company.

Re-engineering and information systems

Connecticut Mutual Life Insurance Co. provides an example of successful business process re-engineering with information systems as the critical com-ponent (Scites, 1993). The company's client services group had traditionally interacted with a variety of fragmented mainframe systems, leading to exces-sively redundant paper generation. The engineering project, named 'One

Image', involved the installation of imaging technology and work flow software to manoeuvre through the various systems, creating the impression of a seamless process. Paper was virtually eliminated, with processing, storage and access to customers' applications being fully automated. As a result, application approvals were significantly accelerated, with a four-fold increase in approvals granted within three days.

IRM from the bottom up

Rockwell Hanford Operations, a division of Rockwell International, undertook a massive plan to integrate the information resources of more than a dozen functional organizations. Unlike many companies, Rockwell took a broad view of information resources, including 'information systems, data processing, telecommunications, information management, and all of the hardware, software, and data processing, that support information exchange' (Corbin, 1986, p. 4). With the objective of improving the productivity of its 5 400 employees, Rockwell devised a bottom-up plan, with user representatives participating from the outset. Top management was firmly committed to the process, and naturally expected to have final approval rights. The involvement of personnel outside the IS department proved to be the key to the system's success, in part because their role gave them a sense of ownership and a vested interest in seeing the plan work, and in part because the resultant system more accurately reflected the reality of their work requirements. The open planning process allowed IS and numerous other departments to design a company-wide management system which was integrated, flexible and easy to use.

Competitive advantage from laser-based information technology

Reading like a Dick Tracy story, McKesson (already a classic textbook example of how to gain competitive advantage through IT) has again revolutionized drug distribution and retailing (Magnet, 1992). Known for introducing electronic linkages with their customer base almost two decades earlier, the drug distributor has added a new twist, using information technology to improve order fulfilment accuracy. Warehousing inefficiencies were causing misfilled orders, irritating customers, and raising operating expenses significantly. The solution came in the form of a wrist-worn laser scanner/computer/radio device. The warehouse worker wearing the device is prompted by a small screen on his wrist for each order to be filled. The system gives the item location, and maps the best route to the appropriate shelf. Once there, the scanner is aimed at a bar-coded shelf tag, which allows the worker to determine if he has the correct item. After gathering the items, the computer radios inventory and billing information to the main computer. In less than seven months, order errors were reduced by 70 per cent, and the associated costs dropped accordingly.

The McKesson case illustrates Strassmann's (1990, p. 330) point that 'information technology makes sense only when it solves a company's specific problems'. In this case, McKesson took a costly problem, order fulfilment, and *151* worked with EDS (Electronic Data Systems) to create the information technology solution required (Magnet, 1992). Indeed, these success stories illustrate the necessity of implementing an information strategy, whether it focuses on information technology alone or on the full spectrum of information resources; one which is based on, and supports, the general business and competitive strategies of the organization. Letting technology drive information management initiatives is akin to putting the cart before the horse, or, to paraphrase McGee and Prusak (1993), the full potential of information technology is only unleashed when users understand how and why they obtain their information, and the IT champions, in turn, understand the full significance and complexity of the user dimension.

A Failed Executive Information System

Kuehn and Fleck (1991) tell the tale of a billion-dollar insurance company which attempted, and failed, to install an executive information system (EIS). The company president, who introduced the idea of an EIS, was committed to the initiative in the belief that it would give his functionally organized firm a competitive edge. A multi-disciplinary task force was established (with personnel from systems, planning, research and development) to develop an EIS capable of supporting senior management's needs. Despite having high-level support, the project stumbled. Early in the evaluation stage, the task force attempted to carry out a cost-benefit analysis. While the costs of creating and maintaining the system were readily identified, the possible benefits were more difficult to classify, and even more so to quantify. As a result, the task force chair recommended that the project not proceed.

Kuehn and Fleck concluded that four factors accounted for the insurance company's failure to implement the EIS:

1   Lack of clear understanding on the president's part of the potential for an EIS in his company's environment.
2   A perception by some functional area heads of the EIS as a threat, and a corresponding failure on the part of the president to stay involved in the project and to communicate to his subordinates his belief in its importance.
3   Too dramatic a swing from a disjointed, transaction-based system to an integrated EIS would likely cost too much, both in money and psychic energy terms for managers using the system.
4   Lack of fit between the structure of the firm and the structure imposed by an EIS, coupled with a lack of understanding by management of the benefits derivable from an EIS.

As Robinson (1992, p. 29) has observed, such IS implementation failures are often attributable to 'logistical, operational, cultural, psychological, and political problems that went unrecognized or unaddressed'.

Information systems crusade

Strassmann (1990, p. 348) provides another case history which underscores the importance of having a forceful product champion, and a strong alignment between an organization's information systems strategy and its business strategy. Houdaille Industries, where the chairman/CEO was convinced that the installation of a materials requirement planning system (MRP) would be a 'crusade for restructuring the business so that he and his staff could understand it in financial terms'. Unfortunately, the necessity of tailoring information systems to the requirements of the firm was not recognized. Houdaille was a manufacturer of machine tools, where a limited number of highly complex, custom-made products was created, a situation in which the skills of highly qualified and flexible craftsmen, capable of making frequent engineering adjustments, mattered greatly. The MRP was unable to reproduce the human element inherent in such work, yet management insisted that its schedules and requirements be adhered to. As a result, the MRP amplified human error and costs began to sky-rocket. Despite pleas from production managers to discard the MRP, senior management continued to believe in its potential. After several years of escalating operating costs, the machine tool division was closed down. In this instance, the IS implementation became more important than the task for which it had been selected. Management's commitment to information technology blinded them to the practical implications of the planned implementation.

ON THE HORIZON

Judging by much of the anecdotal evidence, information technology is as likely to cause iatrogenic dysfunction within organizations as it is to be a panacea. Although it is something of a truism to say that information strategy follows business strategy, the need for alignment is still not always fully recognized at the design and implementation stages of major IS projects. But it's certainly not for want of nostrums in the business/management literature. From Porter's (1985) early work on the role of information technology in competitive strategy to Davenport's (1993) book, *Process Innovation: Re-engineering Work through Information Technology*, the potential of IT to create strategic advantage within organizations has been widely touted. None the less, as we have tried to show, there is within the broader IS community an almost reflexive tendency to think in terms of systems/architectural solutions rather than in terms of an holistic approach to the management of information. This blind spot may well have career implications for IS managers: in Davenport's (quoted in Maglitta, 1994a, p. 77) view, it is possible that 'the bulk of the IS profession will become plumbers' by eschewing what he terms the 'business change/information, high value-added route'.

In much of the information systems/management/science literature, exhortations to adopt a more user/behaviour-centred approach to the design and implementation of information systems have become commonplace, for example Watters and Shepherd's (1994) 'Shifting the Information Paradigm from Data-centered to User-centered'. However, '[h]uman-centered information management', to use Davenport's (quoted in Maglitta, 1994a, p. 72) phrase, requires something extra: 'The ecological view is kind of an orientation to behaviour. It recognizes that there are living, breathing, thinking people who are involved in this information environment. How they use the information, whether they use the information, how they share it, whether they share it starts to be very important.'

No doubt, we can now expect that information ecology's stock will rise dramatically in the months ahead, as, first, the management consulting and then the IS/IM professions latch on to the concept. It is, however, worth noting that an ecological perspective to information was proposed a decade ago by Blake (1985, p. 99), who argued that 'ecology . . . underlies both "information for management" and "management of change"'. The ecological metaphor, of course, was centre-stage in Huberman's (1988) seminal volume, *The Ecology of Computation*. Notwithstanding, we may reasonably expect that information management thinking, ever fuzzy, will attempt to re-anchor itself with the ecological perspective.

REFERENCES

Ball, M.J. and Douglas J.V. (1988), 'Part II. Planning and Implementing Integrated Information Services. Integration and Outreach', *Journal of the American Society for Information Science*, **39** (2), 107–12.

Ball, M.J. and Reese, E.L. (1994), 'Information Services at the University of Maryland at Baltimore: Giving the Vision Life', *Journal of the American Society for Information Science,* **45** (5), 326–30.

Blake, M.L. (1985), 'Information as the Possible', *Journal of Information Science*, **10**, 99–109.

Boaden, R.J. and Lockett, A.G. (1991), 'Information Technology, Information Systems and Information Management: Definition and Development', *European Journal of Information Systems*, **1** (1), 23–32.

British Computer Society (1990), *From Potential to Reality: 'Hybrids' – a Critical Force in the Application of Information Technology in the 1990s*, London: British Computer Society.

Brittain, J.M. and Abbott, W. (eds) (1993), *Information Management and Technology in Healthcare: A Guide to Education and Training*, London: Taylor Graham.

Business Week (1986), 'Management's Newest Star: Meet the Chief Information Officer', 13 October, 160–72.

Central Computer and Telecommunications Agency (CCTA) (1989), *Managing Information as a Resource*, London: HSMO.

Corbin, D.S. (1986), 'Bottom-up IRM Planning: How it Worked at Rockwell', *Information Strategy: The Executive's Journal*, **3** (1), 4–11.

Cronin, B. and Davenport, E. (1991), *Elements of Information Management*, Metuchen, NJ: Scarecrow.

Davenport, T.H. (1993), *Process Innovation: Re-engineering Work through Information Technology*. Boston: Harvard Business School Press.

Dykeman, J.B. (1992), 'Records Management and Top Management: A Win-Win Combination', *Modern Office Technology*, **37** (10), 47.

Earl, M.J. and Skyrme, D.J. (1992), 'Hybrid Managers – What do we Know about Them?', *Journal of Information Systems*, **2**, 169–87.

Feeney, D.F., Edwards, B.R., and Simpson, K.M. (1992), 'Understanding the CEO/CIO Relationship', *MIS Quarterly*, **16** (4), 435–47.

Horton, F.W. and Marchand D.A. (1982), *Information Management in Public Administration*, Arlington, VA: Information Resources Press.

Huberman, B.A. (1988), *The Ecology of Computation*, Amsterdam and New York: Elsevier.

Jones, P. (1994), 'Records Management Renaissance: The UK Local Government Perspective', *Records Management Journal*, **4** (1), 13–19.

Kuehn, R. and Fleck, R.A. (1991), 'Implementing an EIS in a Large Insurance Corporation,' *Journal of Systems Management*, **42** (1): 6–11, 17.

LaPlante, A. (1993), 'Does your Corporate Data Have Market Value?,' *Infoworld*, 25 October, 60.

Library of Congress Subject Headings (1994), 12th edn. Washington, DC: Library of Congress.

McGee, J.V. and Prusak, L. (1993), *Managing Information Strategically*, New York: Wiley.

Maglitta, J. (1994a), 'Information Please', *Computerworld*, **28** (2), 69–72.

Maglitta, J. (1994b), 'Meet the New Boss', *Computerworld*, **28** (11), 80–2.

Magnet, M. (1992), 'Who's Winning the Information Revolution,' *Fortune*, 30 November, 110–17.

Menagh, M. (1994), 'Crossfire', *Computerworld*, **28** (9), 87, 90.

Paez-Urdaneta, I. (1992), 'To Experience a Connection; in Search of a New Information Professional for Latin America', in *State of the Modern Information Professional 1992–1993*, The Hague: FID Special Interest Group on Roles, Careers and Development of the Modern Information Professional, 33-53.

Porter, M.A. (1985), *Competitive Advantage*, New York: Free Press.

Quarstein, V.A., Ramakrishna, H.V., and Vijayaraman, B.S. (1994), 'Meeting the IT Challenge of Business', *Information Systems Management*, Spring, 62–70.

Reponen, T. (1993), 'Strategic Information Systems – A Conceptual Analysis', *Journal of Strategic Information Systems*, **2** (2), 100—4.

Rifkin, G. (1993), 'Ciao for CIOs?' *Forbes ASAP*, 25 October, 93–101.

Roberts, N. and Wilson, T.D. (1987), 'Information Resources Management: A Question of Attitudes?', *International Journal of Information Management*, **7**, 67–75.

Robinson, J.A. (1992), 'The Search for the Technological Panacea', *Information Strategy: The Executives's Journal*, **8** (4), 28–30.

Scites, J.L. (1993), 'Transforming the Dinosaur', *Best's Review*, **94** (7), 76–8.

Shah, J. and Leja, C. (1991), 'Businesses Triumph with IRM', *Information Executive*, **4** (4), 30–4.

Stephens, C.S. (1994), 'The Role of the CIO: A Status Report', *Information Strategy: The Executive's Journal*, **10** (10), 48–51.

Strassmann, P.A. (1990), *The Business Value of Computers*, New Canaan, CT: Information Economics Press.

Synott, W.R. and Gruber, W.H. (1981), *Information Resource Management*, New York: Wiley.

Watters, C. and Shepherd, M.A. (1994), 'Shifting the Information Paradigm from Data-centered to User-centered', *Information Processing & Management*, **30** (4), 445–71.

Conclusion

David P. Best

What conclusions, if any, can we draw from this tour through the field of information management?

First of all, it seems clear that as a discipline, it has some way to go. Although information is coming to be recognized as the priceless resource that it is, the concept of managing it independently of its medium or technology has yet to become fully established.

Second, and perhaps because the distinction between information and medium is so difficult, our concept of the way of using information as part of organizational processes is frequently confused with the manipulation of the media on which it is kept; to understand this distinction in full will enable us to rationalize the use of information in process.

Third, the skills needed, spanning as they do business, information and technology areas, are rare and not yet part of training programmes for managers in MBA and other Business School courses.

Fourth, the economic thinking to enable proper valuation of the resource is as yet uncodified and this contributes to the difficulties expressed above.

Notwithstanding this, the chapters here have also told a number of success stories where the disciplines, techniques and technologies described have been successfully employed to bring about real change in many organizations. From my own practice I know of numerous major corporations as well as departments of central and local government which are benefiting from applying IM principles, and where the challenges discussed here are being successfully tackled.

I hope that this book will provoke and stimulate those who need it to try some of these ideas in the context of their own organizations and perhaps to then contribute their experience to the further development of information management.

The field of information management has never been more exciting than it is today: our pressing needs, the technologies available to us, and the demands of our business, governments and society as a whole present a challenge to us to find ways of satisfying demands for ever more relevant, up-to-date and accurate information at an economic cost. Whether we succeed or fail is up to us.

Appendix
Supplier contacts

PROCESS MODELLING TOOLS

Product	Supplier	Telephone Number
ActionWorkflow Analyst	Quintec International	01268 270 601
Business Design Facility (BDF)	TI Information Engineering	01784 245 058
Business Intelligence facility (BIf)	Virtual Software Factory Ltd (VSFL)	01425 474 484
CASEwise Modeller	CASEwise	0171 722 4000
EIR	Quality Methods Consultancy	01602 243 389
Enterprise Modeller	Business Integration Technologies Ltd	0116 263 0135
IDEF	IDEFine	01344 772 794
IThink	Cognitus Systems Ltd	01423 562 622
Oracle Process Modeller	Oracle	01932 872 020
ProcessWise Workbench	ICL	01344 472 000
Quesheet	Logical Water	01223 846 677
RADitor	Co-Ordination Systems	01602 243 389
SES/workbench	SES UK Ltd	01235 861 321
TOP-IX	TOP-IX Ltd	01789 414642
Witness	AT&T Istel Ltd	01527 550 330
WorkDraw	Edge Software Inc	0101 510 462 0543

Clearly this is only a small selection of the available products. Those requiring further information could usefully contact:

The IOPT Club (Introduction of Process Technology)
PRAXIS plc.
20 Manvers St

BATH
BA1 1PX
0225 444700

Process Product Watch
ENIX Ltd
3 The Green
Richmond
SURREY
44 181 332 0210

Sequent Computer Systems Ltd
Weybridge Business Park
Addleston Road
Weybridge
SURREY
KT15 2UF

Index